Facing Life ... Enjoy the Whether

Ronald Joseph Schinderle

WESTBOW°
PRESS
A DIVISION OF THOMAS NELSON
& ZONDERVAN

WestBow Press books may be ordered through booksellers or by contacting:

WestBow Press
A Division of Thomas Nelson & Zondervan
1663 Liberty Drive
Bloomington, IN 47403
www.westbowpress.com
1 (866) 928-1240

ISBN: 978-1-4908-7914-7 (sc)
ISBN: 978-1-4908-7916-1 (hc)
ISBN: 978-1-4908-7915-4 (e)

Library of Congress Control Number: 2015907097

Print information available on the last page.

WestBow Press rev. date: 04/30/2015

Contents

"FACING LIFE ... enjoy the whether."

At first glance 'whether' seems like a
typo of "Enjoy the weather."

What is 'a whether'? A whether is a turning point in your life
that will determine a change of direction. The road reaches a "T"
and you must go left or right and live with your choice. We all
had 'whethers' that brought us to this point of decision. In the
marketplace you decided whether or not you will buy this book. I
encourage you to enjoy my story as you read for knowledge, added
discernment, and pleasure. Share this book with another person
by having one of you read these pages out loud.

What is the essence of "FACING LIFE ..."? With Abba, Jesus,
and the Holy Spirit I aim to live each new day with Faith, Courage,
and Optimism.

Keep "SAYING SO": keep declaring it and God will do it.

I want my words to change the situation. I am healthy. I am
prosperous. I have the favor of God. I am strong in the Lord. I
am one of a kind. God will add to me ... a spouse!!! I have great
Clarity in my writings. God is going to show me something
that I have never seen. I thank God for His daily Blessings. The
right people are in my future. My heart is receptive. With long
life God is going to satisfy me. (Inspired by 'Rev. Joel Osteen')

"Be well. Be whole. Be full of wisdom. And God bless you."

How do I tell my story?

One of the quotations that has loomed large in my life since 2006 A.D. is this: "People don't care how much you know until they know how much you care."

Chapter 1 – "RAINBOWS" is God and Noah after the flood. For me my horizon involves "25 people" all impacting me for "Good, Better, Best." 'Rainbows in the sky' become memorable. They add beauty and grandeur to any person's day. This book is for anybody and everybody.

This book is intended to be non-judgmental. If some passages motivate you to change, then do not feel threatened. As a 1st born I realize it is common to have perfectionism issues.

I too realize your Time is valuable. I pray this be "a good investment for you."

Discipleship as a Catholic Priest or as a layman Pentecostal begins with "JESUS and the boat." (Chapter 2). Jesus is 'the Master.' He called his 11 apostles and a total of 500 disciples to gather in the Upper Room in Jerusalem and pray for the coming of the Holy Spirit.

I did not become a Catholic Priest or a Catholic Deacon, but the call to follow JESUS is a universal call to all people. "The Great Commission" (MARK 16:15-18) is for you and for me.

Almost all Americans are or have been or will be married. The future (according to 'Dawn') is for hope and for dreams to come true.

"Harvest" (Chapter 3) begins when we speak the right word at the right time. Women seeking friendship seek 'Men of honor, Men of character.' I am growing in Optimism.

The goal in all my writings (from 1980 in Bay City to the present) is to get closer to God and encourage my audience to accept THE THREE IN ONE and build a solid relationship with Him. As I remember past Blessings I take encouragement that THE BEST is on its way. When we smile, we are a living Testimony of God's Love. When I asked 'Dawn' her reaction to last week's pages, she answered: "I like them."

'Pastor Spence,' Stockbridge (Georgia), exhorted: "What have you done today that will make you better tomorrow? There's power in self-investment! Get better!" This Chapter ends with a description of "How I was healed of 25+ years of Chronic Depression."

Big Rapids (Lower Michigan) is "My native city" (Chapter 4). Big Rapids is where I was born, raised, and now reside. My Brother Gary (20 months younger, one grade difference in school) gave me this compliment in 2012: "Your memory is really sharp." The secret that distinguishes professional writing from that of 'the average Joe' is given us by KODAK: *"The genius is in the details."*

What better role model is there than a Dad who smiles so much that his nickname at the golf Country Club is 'Smiley.' He personified Chapter 5 – "Praise God cheerfully." Nothing bothered him. He was always 'Calm' although me changing into my play clothes after my 1st Holy Communion on Mother's Day at age 7 when he wanted "slides on his Kodak Extachrome 127 film" was not the best way to celebrate this Church occasion.

How did I praise God cheerfully? Chapter 5 gives a detailed account of me 'Praising God cheerfully' from a youth to an adult managing schizophrenia related delusions in 2014. PHILIPPIANS 4:6a, 7b – The MESSAGE. "Don't fret or worry instead of worry, pray … It's wonderful what happens when Christ displaces worry at the center of your life."

Every leader for God (Chapter 6) starts as a follower. Whether that leader is a parent, a teacher, a person in sales: education and experience make a difference. What does 'Inspiration' do? It started 'Solomon' on a course of WISDOM. The greater the Wisdom that each person gains, the more productive and successful he and she becomes. What kind of words does a leader for Christ speak? Words of praise, words of appreciation, words of encouragement, words of understanding: these words all SPEAK LIFE.

Chapter 7 is about 'Holiness.' It is also a Biblical treatise on "the joy of the Lord." That means I share Scriptures on JOY, and weave my story on Marriage or 'potential Marriage.' My Pastor, Rev. Joseph N. Cottle,' shepherds this chapter as I and 'Dawn' enjoy the whether. For me: "Faith is Fantastic Adventures In Trusting Him!" God's creatures enhance my joy which I thank the Almighty for. In the presence of God is the fullness of Joy.

"Productivity" (Chapter 8) expands as we build towards greater usefulness for God. In the Marketplace perfectionism gives way to Biblical excellence. My 1st paid job (not counting shoveling snow) was selling "the Pioneer," the Big Rapids newspaper. Then in III – College I started honing my teacher skills. As a Boy Scout I already was developing "Integrity." Productivity in the Kingdom of God occurs whenever a person hears the Word, keeps it, and brings forth fruit with patience. This is what I like about 'Dawn'?

My crowd of "Readers" was small but I kept writing. I am a powerful soul winner. I am a Champion for God.

"Fully Rely on God" (Chapter 9). Are you patient enough to do it God's way? ISAIAH 52:12a – The MESSAGE. "But you don't have to be in a hurry. You're not running from anybody!" God, THE THREE IN ONE, is my Foundational Rock. 'Overflow' is what God blesses you with beyond your thinking and imagination. Certainly, I pray "Blessings to all my Readers!" Your choices of 'whether' will be Godly decisions.

The God of heaven will prosper me … We don't think you will make heaven … Give them your Faith confession … The Lord gave me Favor. In Chapter 10 ("Children of Light"): Get ready for your breakthrough!!!!!

After Breakthrough

According to 'Alice': "There aren't many books written by Catholics."

From 'Nancy S': "You will always be a Catholic in my book." From her husband: "If I can't trust you, Ron, who can I trust?"

From 'Fr. Max J. Frego': "I knew you were a Missionary! Why do you think I sent you all those cards and monetary gifts?"

From 'Padre Fungo' (my Italian name at the Youth Center where I gave my Time): I started as a charismatic Catholic in November 1971 in Rome. I have lived and expect to live as a Pentecostal (non-denominational) since the summer of 1993. It is my belief that GOD is using my efforts (my writings and my life) to bring many souls into the Kingdom.

'ABBA' is the Aramaic for "Father, Daddy."

What happens after Breakthrough? 'Dr. Lester Sumrall' encouraged us: "Be a better person today than you were yesterday. Be more mature in your Christian walk this week than last week."

From 'Dawn': [Enjoy the day!]

What has Jesus the Christ brought us?

'Ellaine' elaborates: "Forgiveness, peace, joy, purpose, satisfaction, fullness, hope, fellowship, freedom, love, power, guidance and light. Praise the Lord."

Rainbow7, FACING LIFE, 4-10-2014

PHILIPPIANS 4:13 – KJV. "I can do all things through Christ which strengtheneth me."

"Let God build you, your reputation, and your career. When the time is right He will deliver you out of adversity, and then you'll see the fulfillment of your dreams." (ENDING YOUR DAY RIGHT, Joyce Meyer – March 31st.)

[Tomorrow is the longest day.]

Taken out of context:

Could it be "Tomorrow is the longest day" because 'the present day' is all that we ever have. Tomorrow is future and according to MATTHEW 6:34 – The MESSAGE: "Give your entire attention to what God is doing right now, and don't get worked up about what may or may not happen tomorrow. God will help you deal with whatever hard things come up when the time comes."

A change of seasons

SONG OF SOLOMON 2:11-12. [KJV]. "For, lo, the winter is past, the rain (the snow) is over and gone; (12) The flowers appear on the earth; the time of the singing of birds is come, and the voice of the turtle is heard in our land;." ("The voice of the turtle" is the cooing of turtle doves.)

From the Wisdom Keys of Dr. Mike Murdock:

"Your Memory Replays The Past; Your Imagination Preplays Your Future." My memory is … already supercharged. I need to begin to nurture my underdeveloped imagination so that … God-facts become the opening to abundant living with THE THREE IN ONE on this earth.

What should we do?

1ST TIMOTHY 6:12 – KJV. "Fight the good fight of faith, lay hold on eternal life, whereunto thou art also called, and hast professed a good profession before many witnesses."

MATTHEW 5:16 – KJV. "Let your light so shine before men, that they may see your good works, and glorify your Father which is in heaven." (Role models)

Each day well lived … with Courage and
Faith gives GOD honor and glory.

[Sweet dreams]

I awoke. My dream surprised me. Before leaving the North American College (Vatican City State) on December 23, 1971 – I worked at the L'oratorio (the Italian youth center in Trastevere). For Christmas 1971 my Mother sent me three Christmas trees to decorate. My friend, Patrizia, received the tallest tree. My morning dream last June (2013) ended with me proclaiming: "My wife is Patrizia." My unmarried friend (mother of three children) who likes the pen name 'Dawn' responded: "I'm all grown up."

The world says, "Worry and Fear."

GOD says: "I am here for you and I love you."

1ST Epistle of John. 1ST JOHN 4:18 – KJV. "There is no fear in love; but perfect love casteth out fear: because fear has torment. He that feareth is not made perfect in love."

From my 1st Cousin Linda:

"We just became proud grandparents of a GIRL! Bryce and Christy named her 'Lily Marie,' 9 pounds 2 ounces. After 3 darling grandsons it was a shock and a delight." (Born on 4-03-2014)

John's Gospel. JOHN 8:32 – KJV. "And ye shall know the truth, and the truth shall make you free."

JOHN 15:2 – The MESSAGE. "I am the Real Vine and my Father is the Farmer. He cuts off every branch of me that doesn't bear grapes. And every branch that is grape-bearing he prunes back so it will bear even more."

THE BIBLE: "Own it. Read it. Live it."

MATTHEW 6:21 – KJV. "For where your treasure is, there will your heart be also."

COLOSSIANS 3:17 – The MESSAGE. "Let every detail in your lives – words, actions, whatever – be done in the name of the Master Jesus, thanking God the Father every step of the way."

My native city

"Big Rapids, Michigan" was originally name 'Leonard.' This lasted for 2 ¾ years in the 1850s. (From: 'John Stilson,' Big Rapids Postmaster, letter of April 8, 2006 to all Postal Patrons)

BOY SCOUTS: from age 11 to 18

The Boy Scout motto is: *"Do a good turn daily."*

My challenge: *"What will I do to help someone today?"*

From 'Dawn': "The future is for hope and for dreams that come true."

Pray about everything!
[Everybody prays differently.]

Further instructions
Be pure, clean, and holy.

In Jesus, all the promises are "Yea and Amen." (2ND CORINTHIANS 1:20). This growth from 'Believing' will turn a life right with God.

Cheerfulness is the beginning of Joy.
[I hope you are happy!] "If you're happy, I'm happy."

Ronald (Wise Ruler) Joseph (God will add …) Schinderle (Chinderle in Austrian) is a Worker in the Kingdom for the King at 'Heaven is for Eternity.' I call it: "Harvest Prosperity."

JOB 8:7 – KJV. "Though thy beginning was small, yet thy latter end should greatly increase."

What goes into 'mental age'?

There are 12 questions centering on these areas: creativity, calmness, flexibility, adventures, relaxation, risk // fun, passion, curiosity, enjoyment, courage, and openness. (Shared by Annie)

Rating myself:

6, 4, 5, 9, 7, 4 // 8, 9, 5, 7, 10, 3 [LOL] ☺ + ☺.

> 'Dawn' as a religious name means "Strong." In Mother Nature it means "like the sun coming out in early morning." For others it means "dish wash soap."

> "Don't be afraid to take a risk."

What does my imagination bring? *Ideas, events, persons!!!*

Basketball coaching: free throw shooting –

Let each player start shooting free throws "two shots." If they score on both, they continue to shoot until they miss or make five in a row. Then they rotate. Try three rotations with "15 points" a perfect score. On another day each player shoots five free throws, then rotates. Try this for five rotations of five shots. The perfect score this time is "25 points."

2ᴺᴰ CORINTHIANS 8:7 – The MESSAGE. "You do so well in so many things – you trust God, you're articulate, you're insightful, you're passionate, you love us – now, do your best in this, too."

We, the Harvest Generation, have God's favor (grace increasing). God's handiwork brings 'Reaped Prosperity' and souls won to everlasting life!

ROMANS 12:1-2. [KJV]. "I beseech you therefore, brethren, by the mercies of God, that ye present your bodies a living sacrifice, holy, acceptable unto God, which is your reasonable service. (2) And be not conformed to this world: but be ye transformed by the renewing of your mind, that ye may prove what is that good, and acceptable, and perfect, will of God."

Humility: 'Pastor Joe and Ann'

"It takes a BIG PERSON to do something small. This is humility ..." (Rev. Joel Osteen, SAY SO – Day 31) 'Pastor Joe and his wife Ann' both escorted 'Remona' to her door. She was then 81-years-old.

What goes into Creativity?

"Problem solving and imagination produce new and better ways of doing things, easier and more profitable ways of doing things." (Steven)

For / from me: "Imagination is … bringing the textbook alive." It involves adaptability: such as a new mixture of old into new fabric designs.

For 'Dawn': How would you rate your Creativity? [a '5' or a '6']

Why is Calmness so valuable?

It gives God the opportunity to answer just as time, place, and people intersect so that He is able to maximize the experience, the Divine Appointment.

Calmness (according to WEBSTER'S SEVENTH NEW COLLEGIATE DICTIONARY) implies freedom from agitation of any sort often in the face of danger or provocation.

The baseball manager or ice hockey head coach who is steady and unshaken no matter what the game situation stabilizes his team.

How is 'Dawn' helping me write meaningful, coherent, realistic pages?

She is sifting "the wheat and the chaff together" and with her ears is elevating my writings so that they will reap a 30-fold, 60-fold, or 100-fold harvest.

JOHN 12:24 – KJV. "Verily, verily, I say unto you, Except a corn of wheat fall into the ground and die, it abideth alone: but if it die, it bringeth forth much fruit."

JOHN 15:5 – KJV. "I am the vine, ye are the branches: He that abideth in me, and I in him, the same bringeth forth much fruit: for without me you can do nothing."

What does Flexibility give you and me?
"I did something different today." (Mary)

When I came out of the seminary (10 1/3 years), I was very 'rigid.' I expected people and events to happen like clockwork. Predictability was my security blanket. Now "newness" goes with "today" to enrich each change of pace. It has been said: "Life is God's novel."

ISAIAH 43:19 – KJV. "Behold, I will do a new thing; now it shall spring forth; shall ye not know it? I will even make a way in the wilderness, and rivers in the desert."

I know travel (World Travel) is at the core of my Adventures.

As I live 2014 my church (Radical Impact Ministries Motivational & Media) no longer has its Sunday Worship at the restaurant "Pepper's Café & Deli" in Big Rapids. Since December 2013 we have met east of Stanwood at Austin Township Hall or at Deerfield Township Hall in Morley. We continue to pray for 'a Building of our own' especially in Big Rapids.

Writing meaningful pages is a daily, weekly challenge. FACEBOOK gets me beyond Big Rapids. It is Ministry I can handle with Jesus' help and by listening to the promptings of the Holy Spirit.

Tidbits about Relaxation

"God's got an interesting sense of humor." (Steven)
"You got guts!" "Gutsy will create beautiful
music." (My Army buddy)

I really enjoy watching and listening to Detroit Tigers Baseball. My Mother taught me to tell time by showing me where the clock hands had to be when I asked her repeatedly, "When does Tigers Baseball come on?"

[Perfect] – Just the right amount of sleep.

"Hiking" - walking in my home town

As a Boy Scout I earned the hiking merit badge. Eight years later in 1970 in Kanderstag, Switzerland, as the hiking merit badge counsellor, I accompanied four Scouts on their 20 mile hike. We walked alongside a mountain lake and then upward to a scenic mountain plateau where the view was 'panoramic,' that is, we had a complete and unobstructed view in all directions!

In Big Rapids it is a 32 minute walk from New Journey Clubhouse to my upstairs apartment. From downtown it is approximately a 30 minute walk to reach my home.

Risk: exposing myself to hazard or danger

Being willing and confident, 'risk taking' expands my horizon in what I strive to do for God. What new adventure do I desire to spruce up my daily activities? How am I interacting with the people God puts in my circle of contacts? In my journey with God I am growing in Patience. 'Pastor Joe' challenged us: "What would you do, attempt to do – if you knew you could not fail?"

In JUDGES 7:1-7 'Gideon' learned that to defeat the Midianites GOD desired all the credit. 'Gideon' did the BIG, the impossible, with 300 men. This was because he listened and obeyed God and gained the Victory only because God intervened.

Earlier in JOSHUA 1:9 – KJV. "Have I not commanded thee? Be strong and of good courage; be not afraid, neither be thou dismayed: for the LORD thy God is with thee withersoever thou goest."

Advice from 'J.M.': Stay genuine, be yourself, and don't copy others. Remember, you are unique.

Fun is Fun is Fun!!

"What are you doing?" I'm thanking God. For what?! The gift of life, new life. For what?! I said, "The gift of love, given by God." For what?! The abundant life, given by our Creator.

Listening hour after hour to "Contemporary Christian music" on my 42 inch HD TV brings "Praise to God" right into my living room. I do not have to wait for monthly 'Community Praise' at Resurrection Life in Big Rapids, the church 'Dawn' attends.

Weekly indoor swimming with my blind friend 'Doug' improves my health. He loves the pool.

2ND CORINTHIANS 5:17 – KJV. "Therefore if any man be in Christ, he is a new creature: old things are passed away; behold, all things are become new."

Passion, fervor, ardor, enthusiasm, zeal

These all mean intense emotion compelling action. When I rated myself on this quality as a '9,' I knew I had a passion for writing. Broadening the scope of this emotion to zeal and enthusiasm boosts my dedication to God's work. Ever since January 2007 I have labored, toiled, devoted my life to serving the King (Jesus Christ of Nazareth – Emmanuel) in the Kingdom.

Curiosity starts with "picking someone's brain."
It does not have to set the world on fire.

This is a modest "5-7-5 syllable" Haiku poem.

Curiosity / An eager desire to learn / Did not kill this Cat

'Dawn' rated her own Curiosity: [I would be a '9' or a '10.' I like to learn.]

Enjoyment for 'Dawn' is: [I like to chill
out] especially after a tiring day.

Enjoyment for me: Finding new Scripture quotes especially in – [KJV], [NKJV], and [The MESSAGE]. Watching and listening to sports highlights. Writing and typing my personal thoughts. Listening to my Christian CDs and DVDs. Many hours of sleep, as caused by my new mix of medications as of my Midland hospitalization for six days (June 28 – July 3, 2013).

Prayer is about the heart responding to God, our Creator and our Sustainer. Intercessory Prayer (petitions) and Soaking Prayer (spending Quality Time with Abba, Father) both increase and foster greater Intimacy with God. He desires a growing interpersonal relationship with each human being.

From 'Co-Pastor Sheron McKinnon-Strong' (God's Prophetic Word Ministries, Chicago): "Answered Prayer is on its way!"

From 'Marla': "Thanks Ron! Hope things are going well for you. Have a great Resurrection Sunday and Spring."

Courage: the opposite of cowardliness

"God will anoint you for something in your #future that doesn't line up with your current condition." (Minister Paula White)

2ND TIMOTHY 1:6 – KJV. "Wherefore I put thee in remembrance that thou stir up the gift of God, which is in thee by the putting on of my hands."

Timothy, stir up the gift from God because you are petrified by fear.

2ND TIMOTHY 1:7 – "With power, love, and a sound mind" you can do about everything.

DANIEL 6:7-24. Daniel was in the lions' den and the true, only GOD protected him.

ACTS 6:5-8; 7:54-60. Stephen became a deacon and was the 1st Christian martyr. He knew he would die, but he continued to witness, boldly proclaiming Jesus as Lord.

"Courage is my friend Ron trying to write a book with all the critics of the world out there." (My Army buddy)

DEUTERONOMY 30:14 – KJV. "But the word is very nigh unto thee, in thy mouth, and in thy heart, that thou mayest do it."

JAMES 4:7-8a. [KJV]. "Submit yourselves therefore to God. Resist the devil, and he will flee from you. (8) Draw nigh to God, and he will draw nigh to you."

For 'Bob': Courage would be "to try something new like visiting a new church or joining a new group."

For the Chicago Cubs: "Courage" is enduring 100 years now at Wrigley Field with no World Series championship. They do fly a 1908 flag for a World Series championship in a different ballpark.

For the Detroit Tigers: "Courage" is disregarding nine straight losses to the Mike Trout Los Angeles Angels. Then losing 11-1 before scoring five runs in the 7th inning at home. The next day Mike Trout took 'the Golden Sombrero' by striking out four times in four at-bats as Detroit won "5-2."

For me: "Courage" is being willing to make a mistake and being man-enough to live with the consequences.

Being courageous means 'being optimistic and SPEAKING LIFE.'

My relationship with God has to be a living, daily connection.

Happy Resurrection Sunday!!!
"He indeed is risen." (Pastor Joe)

In late summer 1973 I entered Kent Oaks Psychiatric Unit in Grand Rapids, Michigan, and stayed seven weeks, diagnosed as "schizophrenia disorder." My Pastor 'Rev. William McKnight' told my Parents that I had suffered 'a personality suicide.' In a 2006 Deliverance Session with 'Pastor James Brandt' he said that I had cursed myself in 1973 when I said "It will take 20 years before I am at the point I desire my personality to be."

It took 25+ years from 1985 to be healed of "Chronic Depression," but in October 2011 after writing Vol. 1 of my autobiography (MOMENT-u-M) I learned that living each day trying to duplicate yesterday was not the right way to live. Now I try to live each day with 'Courage' facing life as "God's novel."

In 2014 the Spirit of the Living God is at work in my life, and I have insight into managing the symptoms of "schizophrenia" and maintaining recovery.

What is the Heart?

The heart pumps blood throughout the human body. According to WEBSTER'S SEVENTH NEW COLLEGIATE DICTIONARY the heart is "the whole personality including intellectual as well as emotional functions or traits."

'Ronald, Knight of the Word': hunger for the Word.

MATTHEW 5:6 – KJV. "Blessed are they which do hunger and thirst after righteousness: for they shall be filled."

AMOS 8:11 – KJV. "Behold, the days come, saith the Lord GOD, that I will send a famine in the land, not a famine of bread, nor a thirst for water, but of hearing the words of the LORD."

A "5-7-5 syllable" Haiku poem expressing
my original lifetime goal:
Diocesan Priest / Bring Scripture alive
to all / Celebrate the Light

How did I mature into 'the Knight of the Word'?

In 9th grade Seminary my Diocesan Priest Religion teacher asked us to name four books of the [OT]. I knew Genesis, Psalms, and Proverbs so I wrote down: 1st Kings, 2nd Kings, 3rd Kings, 4th Kings. Later on I learned that these four books are: 1ST and 2ND SAMUEL, 1ST and 2ND KINGS, 1ST and 2ND CHRONICLES.

In 11th grade during our five day retreat I read my 1st complete Gospel, all 28 chapters of MATTHEW.

In 1st College Monsignor Shaw taught [NT Greek]. Our text was Greek on one side of the page and Latin on the other side. Between 1999 and 2001 Pastor Jim Austin at Christ's Harvest Ministries called me "a walking Bible." In June 2009 I purchased the Amplified Bible paperback. It was in 2012 that 'Pastor Joe' named me: "Sir Ronald, Knight of the Word."

The versions of the Bible that I now own are: [KJV], [NKJV], [NASB], [NIV], [AMP], [NLT] and [The MESSAGE].

Openness: the opposite of close-minded

To me "Openness" represents tolerance to others. "Having my own way" could be a characteristic of selfishness.

JEREMIAH 18:1-6 is the Potter having the final decision into what type of vessel He creates. I am a yielded vessel to the Potter. Because of God's Love I am alive and a contributing member of God's family. I love because He first loved me. Just as there is no other 'me' I have heard that each snowflake is unique. That no other snowflake is the same surprises and amazes me, yet I also know that God named each star in all the galaxies (PSALMS 147:4).

Openness (according to my Army buddy) is being candid and outspoken when ridicule or rejection could result.

"Give God no rest until He establishes you ..." (ISAIAH 62:7)

"Know that what God promised will come to pass in the time that has been promised for its fulfillment!" (Co-Pastor Sheron Strong, Apostolic Truth World Ministries)

"Every day is a great day!"
Everything going WELL with you? Excellent.

PSALMS 118:24-25. [KJV]. "This is the day which the LORD hath made; we will rejoice and be glad in it. (25) Save now, I beseech thee, O LORD: O LORD, I beseech thee, send now prosperity."

"You know I am learning a lot from your pages so I want to say thanks to you for sending me precious word." (Bro. Zafar Masih – Pakistan)

Thank you for your loving encouragement.
Openness – God's vessels
Kind, loving, laughing – after an hour "I like that guy."
"It is not about how *many* people like you. It is
about *who* likes you." (Dr. Mike Murdock)

This is an optimistic "5-7-5 syllable" Haiku poem:

Big white fluffy clouds / God is blessing us
these days / Fourteen hours sunlight

Why did I name this chapter: "Rainbows"?

GOD loves humankind. Prayer helps me live today with Faith, Courage, and Optimism. It leads me beyond today into the future instead of looking backwards into the past.

JESUS and the boat – 1, 4-28-2014

Discipleship starts with the Master and not with us doing our own thing. The person named Jesus the Christ, our Emmanuel, (God with us), calls each person to follow Him. Jesus called many to be His disciples, His apostles. 500 people were invited to the Upper Room to pray for the coming of the Holy Spirit. 120 accepted the 10-day ordeal. Then the Holy Spirit arrived and the Church began. It was Pentecost Sunday.

MATTHEW 4:18-19. [KJV]. "And Jesus, walking by the sea of Galilee, saw two brethren, Simon called Peter, and Andrew his brother, casting a net into the sea: for they were fishers. (19) And he saith unto them, Follow me and I will make you fishers of men."

MARK 1:19 – KJV. "And when he had gone a little farther thence, he saw James the son of Zebedee, and John his brother, who also were in the ship mending their nets."

LUKE 4:4 – KJV. "And Jesus answered him, saying, It is written, That man shall not live by bread alone, but by every word of God."

LUKE 5:3 – KJV. "And he entered into one of the ships, which was Simon's, and prayed him that he would thrust a little from the land. And he sat down and taught the people out of the ship."

What does "fisher of men" require or mean?

LUKE 5:10b – 11. [KJV]. "And Jesus said unto Simon, Fear not; from henceforth thou shalt catch men. (11) And when they had brought their ships to land, they forsook all, and followed him." The miraculous catch of fish provided money for those who continued to fish fish.

'Dawn,' met a co-worker from 20 years ago at a gas station. He remembered her name. Today she is a brunette, not a blonde. I complimented her: "You are as young as you were 20 years ago." She liked that declaration.

Humorous: "Is there a pot of gold at the end of the rainbow? Yes if you are a green leprechaun."

Contemporary Christian music lifts our
spirits and gives praise to God.

JESUS taught us many truths and promised us many blessings, starting with Grace and Divine Mercy. He said He would go away and send the Holy Spirit, the Comforter (John 15:26) to help us. The Holy Spirit is here to guide us into all truth (John 16:13). Jesus announced that with the Holy Spirit we would do even greater works than He did (John 14:12).

From 'Beatrice Agessa': Kenya

Everyday God thinks of you (Psalms 68:19).
Every hour He looks after you (2nd Thessalonians 3:3).
Every minute He cares for you (1st Peter 5:7).
Every second He loves you (Jeremiah 31:3).
Always be strong and courageous (Joshua 1:5-9).

He will never forsake you (Hebrews 13:5).

From 'Debbie':

GOD stills you. Reassures you. Leads you. Enlightens you. Forgives you. Calms you. Encourages you. Comforts you.

Psalms 100 is an exhortation to praise God cheerfully.

PSALMS 100:4 – KJV. "Enter into his gates with thanksgiving, and into his courts with praise: be thankful unto him, and bless his name."

House hunting with 'Pastor Joe':

'Sir Ronald': "Moving the artillery (speaking in Tongues)!! The next 40 minutes are yours."

Karen wrote: "God wins everyday!! We just have to believe and have faith in Him no matter what happens. Glad you guys found a place."

Get out of your comfort zone and do something NEW for God.

1ST CORINTHIANS 15:58 – KJV. "Therefore, my beloved brethren, be ye stedfast, unmoveable, always abounding in the work of the Lord, forasmuch as ye know that your labour is not in vain in the Lord."

1ST CORINTHIANS 15:58 – The MESSAGE. "With all this going for us, my dear, dear friends, stand your ground. And don't hold back. Throw yourselves into the work of the Master, confident that nothing you do for him is a waste of time or effort."

The Great Commission for you and for me:

JOHN 14:31a – KJV. "But that the world may know that I love the Father; and as the Father gave me commandment, even so I do."

Substitute the Christ-like Ronald (or your own name) and live that out as your "Great Commission." (But that the world may know that Ronald loves the Father, and as the Father gave Ronald commandment, even so Ronald does.)

House hunting gratitude:

"It's not what we wanted. It's what God
wanted for us." (Ann M. Cottle)

It is blessed to trust in God.

JEREMIAH 17:7-8. [KJV]. "Blessed is the man that trusteth in the LORD, and whose hope the LORD is. (8) For he shall be as a tree planted by the waters, and that spreadeth out her roots by the river, and shall not see when heat cometh, but her leaf shall be green; and shall not be careful in the year of drought, neither shall cease from yielding fruit."

What did JESUS promise us about Life?

JOHN 10:10 – The MESSAGE. "A thief is only there to steal and kill and destroy. I come so they can have real and eternal life, more and better life than they ever dreamed of."

From 'Dawn': "The future is for hope and for dreams come true." (April 4, 2014)

"Just seeing the smile on her face this morning – She was radiating Joy, Peace, and … confidence for her future." (May 1, 2014)

Relationships

"True men wait! True men respect! True men protect! True men are Godly." (Rev. Shimmy Kotu – South Africa)

Real men age with you: loving, loyal, dedicated, truthful, and caring for you. To them you remain young, vivacious, energetic and attractive.

Get wisdom, get understanding

PROVERBS 4:5-8. [KJV]. "Get wisdom, get understanding: forget it not; neither decline from the words of my mouth. (6) Forsake her not, and she shall preserve thee: love her, and she shall keep thee. (7) Wisdom is the principal thing; therefore get wisdom: and with all thy getting get understanding. (8) Exalt her, and she shall promote thee: she shall bring thee to honour, when thou dost embrace her."

PROVERBS 4:7-8. [The MESSAGE]. "Above all and before all, do this: Get Wisdom! Write this at the top of your list: Get Understanding! (8) Throw your arms around her – believe me, you won't regret it; never let her go – she'll make your life glorious."

"My prayer is that both you and your pastor will live right and be clean and that you will build a wonderful, Christ-like working relationship to preach the gospel as a team." (Dr. Mark T. Barclay)

The three-fold cord that isn't easily broken is Love, Respect, and Trust.

"BE ENCOURAGED TODAY and remember … There is nothing that you will face today that the Lord can't bring you through!" (Co-Pastor Sheron Strong, Apostolic Truth World Ministries)

MATTHEW 9:37 – KJV. "Then saith he unto his disciples, The harvest truly is plenteous, but the labourers are few;"

> Do things God's way: Declare the Word out loud.
> ROMANS 10:17 – KJV. "So then faith cometh by
> hearing, and hearing by the word of God."

Salvation: how does one qualify?

ROMANS 10:8-10. [KJV]. "But what saith it? The word is nigh thee, even in thy mouth, and in thy heart: that is, the word of faith, which we preach; (9) That if thou shalt confess with thy mouth the Lord Jesus, and shalt believe in thine heart that God hath raised him from the dead, thou shalt be saved. (10) For with the heart man believeth unto righteousness; and with the mouth confession is made unto salvation."

My walk of Faith

PSALMS 71:17 – KJV. "O God, thou hast taught me from my youth: and hitherto have I declared thy wondrous works."

PHILIPPIANS 1:6 – KJV. "Being confident of this very thing, that he which hath begun a good work in you will perform it until the day of Jesus Christ."

Today is the Day: the birth of a day!

You say the sun does not shine until early afternoon, yet spring is here in west central Michigan. The clock went "spring forward" on March 9th. "Moving Day" for 'Dawn and me' was Saturday May 3rd. That was the day we upgraded couches, sofas, davenports: me to 'chocolate brown' and Dawn to shiny greenish brown. Next to arrive are the tree buds, soon to pop.

Do we give the name 'Radical Impact Ministries Motivational & Media' back to Pastor Joe and become 'Dynamic Faith Ministries'? What about the green light to begin Church Services at Canadian Lakes (a 20 minute commute from Big Rapids)? We are praying about 'home base.'

"The One Who upgrades the Blessing" is
'Lord God Almighty.'

MATTHEW 20:16b – KJV. "for many be called, but few chosen."
MATTHEW 22:14 – KJV. "For many are called, but few are chosen."

Let us discover 'today.' So the sun is in and out of the clouds. How about a colorful sunset rivaling the 'Aqua A' of my computer screen savers. In the morning it is all sunshine and blue sky. A positive attitude is the start of a GREAT day!! Being a friend of

God allows me, allows you to expect God's surprises as the day progresses.

God blesses us as we live for Him. His provision includes the new as well as the familiar as we embrace His plans and His ways. He expects us to be grateful for His gift of Life. Intimacy with Him leads to Kingdom-building results.

Reflecting why in the past have I dragged my feet,
knowing newness (change) is the norm?

Being in Catholic seminary (pre and post Vatican II) for 10 1/3 years change was subtle until STRESS caught up with me. I did not learn, I did not experience, the cycle of Life of a newborn. The baby constantly grows (from conception, to birth, to teething, to discipline). The young need to know WHY as they ask questions and listen to commands from authority. With me I had no sons or daughters to age with. Not having a wife I was responsible for only myself. Having a mental health disability was 'a personal liability.' Furthermore, I was never in a position to earn a comfortable living for more than one person. Being frugal with my money I got by, living within my means. My one constant was that I really really loved God.

REVELATION 12:11 – KJV. "And they overcame him by the blood of the Lamb, and by the word of their testimony; and they loved not their lives unto the death."

I am, and always have been, a Kingdom-man!!!!!

PROVERBS 16:24 – KJV. "Pleasant words are as an honeycomb, sweet to the soul, and health to the bones." PROVERBS 16:24

– The MESSAGE. "Gracious speech is like clover honey – good taste to the soul, quick energy for the body."

I, 'Ronald Joseph Schinderle,' am called and chosen to join the early Church disciples, apostles as "a fisher of men and women." In order to maintain focus and be of service to the Body of Christ I must take time to 'chill' with the God-head. Fellowshipping with Abba, Emmanuel, and the Paraclete prepares me to share the Good News (the Gospel) with my circle of influence.

Very importantly, I am in remembrance of 2ND CORINTHIANS 3:2 – KJV. "Ye are our epistle written in our hearts, known and read of all men:"

Then there are those I am evangelizing in Pakistan through my 25 pages "JESUS and THE BIBLE" as translated into Urdu in 2012. On Facebook I have over 350 friends that I share with as an online evangelist. This is sowing 'time' into Kingdom-advancement.

From 'Craig': Awesome Ron!! Keep moving upward and forward … And as Paul said "Press forward to the mark that is in Christ Jesus." (cf. PHILIPPIANS 3:14). No better future than in Him!!

Spontaneous Prayer in English

One of my giftings is praying out loud in "Tongues." I am a member of God's artillery in God's Army. I find it very easy "to sound off" in my heavenly Prayer Language. However, when I am in a group setting praying in conversational English is much more difficult. Praying spontaneously in English is far different from repeating Catholic Mass prayers or the rosary. Even praying "The Our Father" is an already formatted prayer.

Why do I struggle in group English praying? Perfectionism, the approval of others: these are fleshly hindrances. Other Pentecostal believers have an easier time of being Biblically spiritual.

Praying out loud in a one-to-one situation is much easier for me. It goes much smoother.

PHILIPPIANS 4:9 – The MESSAGE. "Put into practice what you have learned from me, what you heard and saw and realized. Do that, and God who makes everything work together, will work you into his most excellent harmonies."

PROVERBS 16:20 – KJV. "He that handleth a matter wisely shall find good: and whoso trusteth in the LORD, happy is he."
"God has won the day again!" (Pastor Joe)

JESUS chose His 12 apostles and then sent out 72 disciples to go before Him and announce that 'the Master' was coming to preach "the Kingdom of God." He also told them: Heal the sick and cast out demons.
"LIFE" means 'So Much.'

'Dawn' requested that I become friendlier to our neighbor who I will name, 'Mike.' He is a computer whiz, has a young daughter, and works midnights. Both 'Dawn and Mike' moved in around September 2012.

DANIEL 11:32b – KJV. ": but the people that do know their God shall be strong, and do exploits."

1ST THESSALONIANS 5:14 – KJV. "Now we exhort you, brethren, warn them that are unruly, comfort the feebleminded, support the weak, be patient toward all men."

One of the characteristics of people with 'schizophrenia' is delusional thinking. Grandiose ideas are representative of such thinking. I was guilty of such thinking as far back as the 6th grade at St. Mary's School. My fantasy then was to be the Pope when Jesus returns. In high school as a junior my Priest friend, Father Max Joseph Frego, bet me $5 that I would study for Catholic priesthood in Rome, Italy. He wanted me to think 'Potential.' I paid that obligation with a fancy luncheon in Lansing, Michigan on a December 30th.

ROMANS 12:3 – KJV. "For I say, through the grace given unto me, to every man that is among you, not to think of himself more highly than he ought to think: but to think soberly, according as God hath dealt to every man the measure of faith."

"LIFE" means 'So Much.'

No matter what your medical diagnosis there is Hope in your future. God does not waste experiences. He allows you to use them to give 'a Testimony.' Smiles, laughs, HUGS: these are constants for confident, healthy people.

JOSHUA 1:9 – KJV. "Have not I commanded thee? Be strong and of a good courage; be not afraid, neither be thou dismayed: for the LORD thy God is with thee whithersoever thou goest."

MATTHEW 25:23 – KJV. "His lord said unto him, Well done, good and faithful servant; thou hast been faithful over a few things, I will make thee ruler over many things: enter thou into the joy of thy lord."

God has a bigger plan for me than I ever dreamed of. I must be patient. Do my homework. Get ready to walk on water like 'Simon Peter' did. This means I expect God to do 'the impossible.' That is what Faith is, and what Faith accomplishes. I believe God has a future for me surpassing all the GOOD of my first 67 years on Earth.

This prophecy of Spencer T. O'Neal ('Pastor Spence' to his congregation in Stockbridge, Georgia) is motivational meat for me: "The way you handle your gift will determine the level of success that you will have. Keep honing your gift and your gift will make room for you. I declare and decree that you will become a hot commodity in high demand." … "Go ahead and praise Him with your gifted self."

"Success" for you and for me "is located at the intersection of preparation and opportunity." (Pastor Spence)

"Every author's success story begins with a leap of faith."
(WestBow Press, A Division of Thomas Nelson
& Zondervan, Christian Publishers)

"If God is in control, we don't have to be." (THE
MESSAGE // REMIX: SOLO – Day 160)

We use the Name, the Blood, and the Word and we PUSH, PUSH, PUSH until we win. (Dr. Terry L. Mize)

PSALMS 25:3a – The MESSAGE. "I've thrown in my lot with you; You won't embarrass me, will you? Or let my enemies get the best of me?"

PSALMS 36:5-6. [The MESSAGE]. "God's love is meteoric, his loyalty astronomic, His purpose titanic, his verdicts oceanic. (6) Yet in his largeness nothing gets lost; Not a man, not a mouse, slips through the cracks."

GALATIANS 6:14 – The MESSAGE. "For my part, I am going to boast about nothing but the Cross of our Master, Jesus Christ. Because of that Cross, I have been crucified in relation to the world, set free from the stifling atmosphere of pleasing others and fitting into the little patterns that they dictate."

"YOU'RE GOING TO BE BLESSED BEYOND YOUR WILDEST DREAMS AND IMAGINATION!!!"

(Co-Pastor Sheron Strong, Apostolic Truth World Ministries)

From 'Dawn': "You have to follow your heart and listen to God." Nothing done for God is a waste of time or energy.

Jesus is our Brother and ultimate role model.

2ND CORINTHIANS 10:5b – KJV. " ...and bringing into captivity every thought to the obedience of Christ."

2ND CORINTHIANS 10:5 – The MESSAGE. "We use our powerful God-tools for smashing warped philosophies, tearing down barriers erected against the truth of God, fitting every loose thought and emotion and impulse into the structure of life shaped by Christ."

My ministry: helping others to appreciate Jesus the Christ

Whether I share Scripture on my Timeline on FACEBOOK or react in a written way to my 350+ Friends on FACEBOOK, I put 'the Master' at the center of their lives.

In this manuscript "FACING LIFE …" I am a literary evangelist for my audience, a real fisherman for men and women from all countries. I also feature my ongoing relationship with 'Dawn.' Both her Dad and her Grandpa were writers. For those interested in my native town (Big Rapids, MI) and its progression as I aged I include "My native city." My Pastor, 'Rev. Joseph N. Cottle,' named me: "Sir Ronald, Knight of the Word."

My story includes seminary recollections of both 'pre and post Vatican II,' my ongoing battle to overcome schizophrenia, my healing in October 2011 from 25+ years of 'chronic depression,' and my own daily devotional materials.

According to a Christian magazine men need: "Faith, Family, Fitness, Finances, and Sports." I am a Major League Baseball enthusiast. On "Jim Leyland Day" the Detroit Tigers Manager (2006 – 2013) responded: There is "a lot less stress" these days.

PSALMS 37:4 – KJV. "Delight thyself also in the LORD; and he shall give thee the desires of thine heart."

LUKE 12:31 – KJV. "But rather seek ye the kingdom of God; and all these things shall be added unto you."

Who am I? According to 'Pastor Joe': "Ronaldus Magnus"

MATTHEW 13:52 – KJV. "Then said he unto them, Therefore every scribe which is instructed unto the kingdom of heaven is like unto a man that is an householder, which bringeth forth out of his treasure things new and old."

MATTHEW 13:52 – The MESSAGE. He said, "Then you see how every student well-trained in God's kingdom is like the owner of a general store who can put his hands on anything you need, old or new, exactly when you need it."

These two accounts lift my confidence as I give the appropriate Scripture verse(s) when needed. As far back as 1999 or 2001 A.D. (Anno Domini – in the year of the Lord) 'Pastor Jim Austin' at Christ's Harvest Ministries called me: "a walking Bible."

> "Giving honor to those who are worthy
> of honor" – Rev. David Stanski.

God gave honor to women. GENESIS 1:27 – God created both male and female in His own image and likeness.

'The Word' gave honor to women. MATTHEW 28:5-10. Jesus appeared to women before He appeared to His apostles.

Jesus gave honor to women. LUKE 10:38-42. (Martha and Mary).

The Church gave honor to women. PROVERBS 31:10-31. (The virtuous wife). EPHESIANS 5:25 – Husband + Wife.

> What is the goal of soul-winning? "The lost get saved."
> Lord, I need You.

PSALMS 18:46 – KJV. "The LORD liveth; and blessed be my rock; and let the God of my salvation be exalted."

Meditation Time: Concentrate on God! Talk to Him.
"I will pray that God blesses you tremendously."
Thank God for answering our prayers.

The Ships of Scripture were dependent on oars and sails for propulsion. The ships of ACTS 21:1-6; 27:6-44; and 28:11-13 were capable of carrying many people and much freight. (Teachers Edition of the Bible, published by A.J. Holman Company – Bible Dictionary Concordance, copyright 1942)

Why did I name this chapter: "JESUS and the boat"?

Jesus explained 'the Kingdom of God.' His fishermen proclaimed the Truth of Jesus after the Holy Spirit filled them on Pentecost Sunday (50 days after Resurrection Sunday).

Furthermore, the Church is 'the boat.'

When somebody says: "We are all in the same boat" this implies that even though circumstances may not be favorable they are the same for each of us or for all of us.

'Dawn' likes the comfort "boats" provide for recreational usage.

Many of my 'Aqua A' screen savers for my Windows 7 tower showcase one or four boats at sunset.

The example of Jesus

MARK 4:35-41. Jesus instructed His apostles to cross the lake, and He fell asleep in the back of the boat. When the storm raged they woke Jesus and He calmed the sea. He certainly was not planning for the boat to go to the middle of the lake and sink.

MATTHEW 14:22-33 records the story of Peter walking on the water to Jesus.

JOHN 21:1-14. After Jesus' Resurrection He appeared to His apostles for the 3rd time at the sea of Tiberias. And it was Simon Peter who hauled 153 fish to land.

Harvest – 1, 5-14-2014

JAMES 1:5 – KJV. "If any of you lack wisdom, let him ask of God, that giveth to all men liberally, and upbraideth not; and it shall be given him."

Every success story starts with WISDOM.

That is what 'Solomon' asked GOD for and GOD was very pleased. 'Solomon' became the richest man that ever lived, even greater than 'Job.'

God will make a way for me.

Why do I say that? First of all, He gives grace and divine mercy to everyone. For me, I gave my life wholeheartedly as an adult to Him on Saturday 18 December 1971 in St. Peter's Basilica, Vatican City State. That lifetime commitment has developed into a progressing friendship with God for over 40 years. Now I like to hang out with Him on a daily basis. According to Rev. Joel Osteen I will have what I "SAY SO."

Exhortation to well being

GALATIANS 6:7 – KJV. "Be not deceived; God is not mocked: for whatsoever a man soweth, that shall he also reap."

Reaping what I sowed: "Happy Mother's Day!"
"Happy Family Day!"

What are these pages 'sowing'?

ISAIAH 52:7 – KJV. "How beautiful upon the mountains are the feet of him that bringeth good tidings, that publisheth peace; that bringeth good tidings of good, that publishes salvation; that saith unto Zion, Thy God reigneth!"

A GOOD RELATIONSHIP is when someone ACCEPTS your Past, SUPPORTS your Present, and ENCOURAGES your Future. This is what 'Dawn and I' are working towards.

Praying for 'Dawn.' Praying for 'Dawn.' Praying for 'Dawn.'
'Select Great Lakes honey' comes from clover.

What Scripture promises 'Success' as a guide
to accomplishing "Destiny Goals"?

JOHN 8:32 – KJV. "And ye shall know the truth, and the truth shall make you free." The Scripture is Truth, both [OT] and [NT].

PHILIPPIANS 4:8 – KJV. "Finally, brethren, whatsoever things are true, whatsoever things are honest, whatsoever things are just, whatsoever things are pure, whatsoever things are lovely, whatsoever things are of good report; if there be any virtue, and if there be any praise, think on these things."

PHILIPPIANS 4:8 – The MESSAGE. "Summing it all up, friends, I'd say you'll do best by filling your minds and meditating on things true, noble, reputable, authentic, compelling, gracious

– the best, not the worst; the beautiful, not the ugly; things to praise, not things to curse."

"PHILIPPIANS 4:8 – KJV" was the 1st Scripture I posted on my bathroom mirror. It remained there until this apartment was remodeled in March 2011. That meant it was visible for eight years.

The right word at the right time

PROVERBS 15:23 – KJV. "A man hath joy by the answer of his mouth: and a word spoken in due season, how good is it!"

LAMENTATIONS 3:25 – KJV. "The LORD is good unto them that wait for him, to the soul that seekest him."

"Men of honor, Men of character":

I want to encourage you gals and you guys. (Rebecca St. James, born July 26, 1977 in Australia)

I am optimistic. I am optimistic.

This is a real plus for me. After 25+ years of 'chronic depression,' healing in October 2011, I remained negative-minded way too often. With this Chapter focusing on "Harvest" I am thankful that my typed pages are flowing freely with GOOD insights and appropriate Scripture.

According to 'Dawn': a balanced life for women depends on age. A 20-year-old needs God and finances. An older woman needs GOD first, then her husband, then her children.

As we "SAY SO" realize that our words are power packed and creative. Yes, bridle the tongue. Speak positives – Speak Life. You shall declare a thing and it shall be established. This is offensive prayer. Defensive prayer is holding the line (football), preventing the opposition from scoring (baseball), and holding the devil captive (spiritual warfare). Focus on thanksgiving and praising God with an open heart.

EPHESIANS 4:29 – KJV. "Let no corrupt communication proceed out of your mouth, but that which is good to the use of edifying, that it may minister grace unto the hearers."

EPHESIANS 4:29 – The MESSAGE. "Watch the way you talk. Let nothing foul or dirty come out of your mouth. Say only what helps, each word a gift."

Try laying on your back on your couch and lift your arms upward. Listen for God to speak to you. I am like a sheep (Psalms 42:5 and Psalms 43:5) that is cast down, its feet (my arms) extending towards the sky. I am listening to the rain pounding down outside my windows. It was not long before God rescued me. 6:46 a.m. – 'Patrizia time.' Peach tea.

1ST JOHN 4:18 – The MESSAGE. "There is no room in love for fear. Well-formed love banishes fear. Since fear is crippling, a fearful life – fear of death, fear of judgment – is one not yet fully formed in love."

2ND PETER 3:18 – KJV. "But grow in grace, and in the knowledge of our Lord and Saviour Jesus Christ. To him be glory both now and for ever. Amen."

Defensive prayer is a prayer to protect. It protects by covering with the blood of Jesus. It wraps the Arms of Jesus around you and your loved ones. Prayer is the best armor for all trials. Where is your heart?

GENESIS 8:22 – KJV. "While the earth remaineth, seedtime and harvest, and cold and heat, and summer and winter, and day and night shall not cease."

EPHESIANS 6:8 – KJV. "Knowing that whatsoever good thing any man doeth, the same shall he receive of the Lord, whether he be bond or free."

From 'Dawn': "Thank you for your prayers."

The goal in all my writings is to get closer to God in my relationship with Him. At the same time my writings should also draw my audience nearer to our Creator and Lord. The Master is glorified when people respond from the heart telling Him that they love and appreciate His presence and His deeds. This advances the Kingdom.

The principle of sowing and reaping

2ND CORINTHIANS 9:6-7. [KJV]. "But this I say, He which soweth sparingly shall reap also sparingly; and he which soweth bountifully shall reap also bountifully. (7) Every man as he purposeth in his heart, so let him give; not grudgingly, or of necessity: for God loveth a cheerful giver."

2ND CORINTHIANS 9:7 – The MESSAGE. "I want each of you to take plenty of time to think it over, and make up your own mind what you will give. That will protect you against sob stories and arm twisting. God loves it when the giver delights in the giving."

Don't be anxious. Pray. Put and keep
CHRIST at the center of your life.

PHILIPPIANS 4:6-7. [The MESSAGE]. "Don't fret or worry. Instead of worrying, pray. Let petitions and praises shape your worries into prayers, letting God know your concerns. Before you know it, a sense of God's wholeness, everything coming together for good, will come and settle you down. It is wonderful what happens when Christ displaces worry at the center of your life."

PHILIPPIANS 4:7 – KJV. "And the peace of God, which passeth all understanding, shall keep your hearts and minds through Christ Jesus."

Warning: IF you keep feeding your mind with negative thoughts, you will live in fear.

2ND TIMOTHY 1:7 – KJV. "For God hath not given us the spirit of fear; but of power, and of love, and of a sound mind." My Pastor, 'Rev. Joseph N. Cottle,' had me praying this verse three times a day as I took short walks for two months during the summer of 2013.

What do I intend to do with these pages, these chapters?

DEUTERONOMY 32:2-3. [KJV]. "My doctrine shall drop as the rain, my speech shall distil as the dew, as the small rain upon the tender herb, and as the showers upon the grass: (3) because I will publish the name of the LORD: ascribe greatness unto our God."

"Good Morning! I'll be handling all your problems today. So, relax and enjoy the day!" Who is speaking in this greeting? "Love, God. P.S. I LOVE YOU!!!" (God is speaking.) Do you believe and expect God to take care of all your details each day? Just give Him a chance: you'll be greatly amazed, as I am, as today has unfolded.

What is Paul the apostle's Great Commission, Great Admission?

1ST CORINTHIANS 1:17-18. [KJV]. "For Christ sent me not to baptize, but to preach the gospel: not with wisdom of words, lest the cross of Christ should be made of none effect. (18) For the preaching of the cross is to them that perish foolishness; but unto us which are saved it is the power of God."

1ST CORINTHIANS 2:4-5. [KJV]. "And my speech and my preaching was not with enticing words of man's wisdom, but in demonstration of the Spirit and of power: (5) That your faith should not stand in the wisdom of men, but in the power of God."

What does 'sowing' produce? Choose your favorite Biblical translation:

I have [KJV], [NKJV], [NASB], [NIV], [NLT], [Amplified], and [The MESSAGE].

JESUS gives the meaning of three Harvest stories:

MATTHEW 13:18-23. Study this story of the farmer planting seed: on the road, in the gravel, in the weeds, on good earth.

MATTHEW 13:24-30. Another farmer's story: the good seed and the thistles (tares and wheat).

MATTHEW 13:31-32. Here we have the story of the growth of the mustard seed.

What about the goodness of God in my life?
Yes, 'Dawn,' I love you but GOD LOVES YOU THE MOST.
"Let God bless you always."
We will survive and God's Best is far better
than we can hope or imagine.
Pray that 'More Harvest' comes.

"Winning and discipling souls for the Kingdom" is the assignment of Catholic Priests, especially those who are chosen to study in Rome. As such a student I studied at the Gregorian University. At THE GREG all the students at the North American College aimed to get every classmate a passing grade ("6.0" on a scale of "1-10") in every course. Exams could be written or oral with no more than 70% one way. All the written potential exam questions were in a booklet in Latin. Semester exams were held at the end of January and the middle of June.

Teamwork was essential. Tape recorder people attended the Monday, Tuesday, Thursday, Friday Italian morning lectures. Translators transcribed the Italian into English. I was one of the typists. Collators copied the typed English pages and made sure each student had the class notes. After the 1st month I did not attend the lectures.

'Being a loner'

School started in mid-October with an all-school
"Opening Mass." I was not in the choir. In my 3rd year
because I chose to remain in the back I became chosen
to be 'a gift bearer at the Offertory time.' Four of us two
by two carried forward the bread and wine. I carried
hosts for Holy Communion. It was a Mass in Latin.
"Pax tecum." Peace be with you personally.
"Pax vobiscum." Peace be with you as a group.

As a loner: I was the only seminarian in my class to work with the
pre-teens at the Catholic Youth Center in 'Trastevere.' I was there
every Monday from 3:30-6:00 PM. On my 1st Monday the Nuns
in charge gave me, 'Padre Fungo,' a sheet of Italian swear words.
That was the only Italian I needed to memorize immediately so I
could supervise the youngsters.

In November 1971 my Mother sent me two small and one large
Christmas trees with decorations to share with the children at
the playground. I was overjoyed when I learned that "Patrizia"
was awarded the tallest, largest tree!

Theology and my limited Italian: "Tu" + "io" = "L'oratorio."

Translation: "You + Me" = "the Church."

One of the translations of "Padre Fungo" is 'Fr. Mushroom.'

From 'Pastor Joe': "You're a good man."

In my 2 1/3 years at "L'oratorio" 'Padre Fungo,' (me) stood 6'1"
and weighed 145 pounds. I wore black pants, a black clerical shirt,

and inserted the traditional Roman collar. The plural of 'Fungo' is "funghi" – mushrooms.

My education through TRAVEL far surpassed my high school expectations. In Italy I visited 'Pope Paul VI' at Castelgondolfo. Then I visted Naples, Assisi, Siena, Florence, Venice, and Sicily. Switzerland was most gracious: both Kanderstag and Lugano. West Germany included the 1970 Passion Play at Oberammergau. France's best was Paris and the stain glass at the Cathedral in Chartres. Then there was 3 ½ days of London theatre and meals to prepare me for a month of India's cuisine. Egypt meant Cairo, the Gizeh Pyramids, and Luxor (the Valley of the Kings and the Valley of the Queens). Traveling outside the U.S.A. exposed me to new cultures, different standards of living, and foreign religions.

JOSHUA 24:15c – KJV. ": but for me and my house, we will serve the LORD."

Personal Healing

PSALMS 107:20 – KJV. "He sent his word, and healed them, and delivered them from their destructions." My friend, 'Tia,' confessed this Scripture and was healed of cancer at a young age.

My Case Manager at Community Mental Health evaluated me, saying: "Your schizophrenia is under control. Enjoy life and keep doing what you have been doing."

Tell us more about the goodness of God in your life.

Without Him there would be no "me." I would not have been conceived. Without his Love I would not have outlived the 66 years of my Dad on Earth. In fact, my friend 'Father Max J. Frego' did think it was me who died in September 1986 when he heard the transcribed message on his answering machine: "Schinderle died."

My present assignment

I am to share peace, joy, and agape love – with whomsoever I am with and in whatever places I find myself. I am blessed to be a blessing through Jesus' provision.

A Ministerial Prayer: Be blessed beyond
all your expected gains for Christ.

From 'Co-Pastor Sheron Strong': "What's to come is so much GREATER & BIGGER than what's been!!!!!" As I, Ronald, remember past blessings I take encouragement that THE BEST is on its way. Yeah and Amen.

Waking up in the morning

There are two kinds of morning people: those that meet God, "Good morning, God!" and those that awake muttering, "Good God, morning?" What type of person are you?

God will give you the words. God will give you the words.

MARK 13:11 – KJV. "But when they shall lead you, and deliver you up, take no thought beforehand what ye shall speak, neither do ye premeditate: but whatsoever shall be given you in that hour, that speak ye: for it is not ye that speak, but the Holy Ghost."

Do 'u' or 'U' need an infusion of Joy?

JOHN 15:11 – KJV. "These things have I spoken unto you, that my joy might remain in you, and that your joy might be full." To gain the context and a fuller meaning of this text do read out loud JOHN 15:1-10.

DEUTERONOMY 1:11 – KJV. "The LORD God of your fathers make you a thousand times so many more as ye are, and bless you, as he hath promised you!"

"You should never sacrifice these three things: your family, your heart, your dignity." (A Facebook photo from 'Ellaine' – Durban, South Africa)

Let's grow in Hope.

Take one day at a time, have a plan, then turn the day over to God's care and trust Him for the outcome.

When you (I) smile, we are a living Testimony of God's Love.

Friendship is not about who you've known the longest. It's about who walked into your life, and said, "I'm here for you," and proved it. (Thanks 'Pastor Joe and Ann')

My heavenly healing from schizophrenia began in church.

In the summer of 2010 Christ's Harvest Ministries had a potluck Wednesday supper followed by 7-8 p.m. Bible Study every week. I had joined "CHM" in September 1994, and my biggest accomplishment was perfect attendance at midweek Prayer and

Sunday morning Worship. The preaching for 16 years did not cause my spiritual growth spurt.

That summer of 2010 'Christopher P. Nicholson' drove me to and from "CHM" to "Shiloh Pines" arriving at 8:40, halfway through Pastor Joseph Cottle's Wednesday night Church Service. At one of those meetings I asked for personal prayer. As 'Pastor Joe' and those dozen prayer warriors interceded my eyes were OPENED spiritually, and I began seeing "Color" in the room and later outside in nature in a brand new way!!!! I began to Smile.

How is my healing from schizophrenia progressing in 2014?

PSALMS 20:6 – The MESSAGE. "That clinches it – help's coming, an answer's on the way, everything's going to work out."

Pastor Joe knows I appreciate 'Instrumental Music' – thus he recommended that I listen to "Light Classical" on my Charter Communications Digital Music. This augments my "Contemporary Christian" that is already a favorite on my new 42 inch HD TV.

Courage: "FACING LIFE …" one day at a time!

"Today, I believe God is doing things for you that you cannot do for yourself! He wants to surprise you with His goodness and amaze you with His love!" (Victoria Osteen – My comment: Thank you for SAYING SO.)

"I let go and know that God always gives me that which is most appropriate for my soul." (Ellaine)

Spiritual growth takes place as we listen and obey the commands of Scripture as Scripture does not change. (HEBREWS 13:8 – KJV. "Jesus Christ the same yesterday, and to day, and for ever.")

While the world relies on "Luck" – the word is derived from the name 'Lucifer': I pray that 'Dawn' receives "Phenomenal bliss."

Assignment Scriptures

PROVERBS 3:27 – KJV. "Withhold not good from them to whom it is due, when it is in the power of thine hand to do it."

1ST THESSALONIANS 5:18 – KJV. "In every thing give thanks: for this is the will of God in Christ Jesus concerning you."

COLOSSIANS 3:17 – KJV. "And whatsoever ye do in word or deed, do all in the name of the Lord Jesus, giving thanks to God and the Father by him."

Born-again

I am very valuable to God. You are very valuable to God. The devil does not like it because God's grace and mercy endures forever. God created us to have Intimacy with Him in heaven, and our heaven begins as soon as we become 'born-again.' In JOHN'S GOSPEL, chapter 3, Jesus the Master educated Nicodemus a Pharisee concerning our new birth.

JOHN 14:6 – KJV. "Jesus saith unto him, I am the way, the truth, and the life: no man cometh unto the Father, but by me."

Graduation

Another type of Harvest is "graduation." It could be from kindergarten, 5th grade, 8th grade, high school, college, or graduate school. We all know the effort that goes into learning. Perhaps forgotten are all those who earn a G.E.D. degree instead of a high school diploma. Also how about those who go back to school later in life and get re-trained for new job opportunities and blessings? "Holy Spirit, fill my heart to overflowing."

Seed-Faith:

LUKE 6:38 – KJV. "Give, and it shall be given unto you; good measure, pressed down, and shaken together, and running over, shall men give into your bosom. For with the same measure that ye mete withal it shall be measured to you again."

"Hi Ronald, I see God is still blessing you with abundance of kindness." (Pamelar)

Getting ready for 'More Harvest':

"What have you done today that will make you better tomorrow? There's power in self-investment! Get better!" (Spencer T. O'Neal, 'Pastor Spence,' Stockbridge, GA)

As long as it takes: retrieving my only [KJV] from Six Lakes Bible Study

PSALMS 70:1 – KJV. "Make haste, O God, to deliver me; make haste to help me, O LORD."

PSALMS 71:1 – KJV. "In thee, O LORD, do I put my trust: let me never be put to confusion."

Bea's friend, 'Roosevelt,' (now my friend)
let me use his [KJV] for seven days.

PSALMS 73:28 – KJV. "But it is good for me to draw near to God: I have put my trust in the Lord GOD that I may declare all thy works."

Church Pastors are overseers of souls. They must live the sermons or homilies that the Holy Spirit inspires them to preach. As shepherds they look to Jesus, the Chief Shepherd, for insight, unity – oneness, and … leadership skills. A sensitivity to people's ongoing needs helps Pastors teach timely messages. Churches that follow a Lectionary are more rigid in what the sermon or homily touches upon. It is the responsibility of congregations to pray and intercede for their Shepherds. Shepherds too also must pray for their flocks.

From the Apostle Paul

PHILIPPIANS 4:9 – KJV. "Those things, which ye have both learned, and received, and heard, and seen in me, do: and the God of peace shall be with you."

The OT Blessing Prayer:

NUMBERS 6:24-26. [KJV]. "The LORD bless thee, and keep thee: (25) The LORD make his face shine upon thee, and be gracious unto thee: (26) The LORD lift up his countenance upon thee, and give thee peace."

How was I Healed from 'Chronic Depression'?

I prayed and believed and acted on MARK 11:24. I spoke and wrote – I believe I have received my healing. Thou hast healed me. I do not consider what I feel. I believe I am healed. Thou hast healed me.

On Tuesday 25 October 2011 at "Shiloh Pines" 'Bishop Caleb Don Crigger' prayed for me. I felt a release in my belly. Seven days later I read from 'Chaplain Mark Haley': "Depression is living in the past." This was exactly what I needed to hear. Now I live in the present the best that I am able. Then I live the next day with newness, justice, and joy.

What did 'Martin Luther' learn from 'Staupitz'?

'MARTIN LUTHER' learned that "repentance begins with the love of God." 'Staupitz' enabled LUTHER to relax, to look at Christ on the cross, not on the judgment seat.

Reportedly, Jesus Christ of Nazareth was born on September 24th. For years my perfectionism thought it takes "Nine months exactly to the day" for a baby to be conceived and carried full-term in the Mother's womb. This means that 'the Harvest' of Christmas Eve, Christmas, and the Feast of St. Stephen – the 1st Christian martyr (December 24, 25, 26) is September 24, 25, 26.

"Salvation is free but discipleship costs
everything you have." (Rev. Billy Graham)

PROMOTION

PSALMS 75:6-7. [KJV]. "For promotion cometh neither from the east, nor from the west, nor from the south. (7) But God is the judge: he putteth down one, and setteth up another."

"^5 and Amen." (KZS)

"Rejoice in the Lord, for he has done a great thing." (My older spiritual son, 'Pastor Elijah')

So I started with ... Mark 11:22-24. That lead to healing from 25+ years of "chronic depression" as a mountain was removed for my future joy and hope.

My native city (Big Rapids, Michigan)

"Big Rapids, Michigan," located in West Central Lower Michigan, was originally named 'Leonard.' This lasted for 2 ¾ years in the 1850s. (From: 'John Stilson,' Big Rapids Postmaster, letter of April 8, 2006 to all Postal Patrons)

BOY SCOUTS from age 11 to 18.

The Boy Scout motto is: *"Do a good turn daily."*

My challenge: *"What will I do to help someone today?"*

> On my 1st camping trip I showed "fear,"
> the opposite of Courage.

It was in the spring of 1958, 5th grade, and we paired off for food. My African-American partner brought foot long hotdogs. We pitched 'Camp' after school on Friday. On Saturday night there was a tornado warning and we were camping on a hillside (rolling terrain) with a small creek in the middle of it. I took the option and chose to go back home for a bath and a good night's rest. In the morning I served Mass and re-joined my Troop 117. After Mass we cooked breakfast of bacon and eggs. Two of us were 'sissies,' choosing to go home for the night. My African-American was a "con-artist." He jumped four feet from the bridge into the creek for money. Actually, we were not total 'sissies.' We did not use plastic silverware and paper plates. We each had our own 'mess kits' and we washed our dishes including our metal silverware.

Q. Why did my father say that they chose to live in Big Rapids?

A. It provided a Catholic Church and School, a college (now named 'Ferris State University'), a hospital, a library, and a chance to work with the "Worcester & Worcester Law Firm." Later he became the Big Rapids city attorney for 33+ years.

PSALMS 127:3-4. [KJV]. "Lo, children are an heritage of the LORD: and the fruit of the womb is his reward. (4) As arrows are in the hand of a mighty man; so are children of the youth."

Q. What do children need?

A. "Prayers for Safety, Peace, Health, Strength, Love, Joy and Direction in Jesus Name. And that the Power of the Holy Spirit Protect them and that they will hear the still small voice of God." (Ron-Romona Dancz, owners & operators of 'East Bay General Store,' Chippewa Lake)

During the summer of 1952 (age 5) we moved from the house on the hill where 'The Ferris Ice Arena' is now a National Landmark. At that time the garage was under the south portion of the house. We moved to our house on Marion Avenue, the home my Mother kept up for 49 years. The location was ideal: just a block and a half from St. Mary's Church and School.

What was 'Special' about 2nd grade?

We had 'Sister Mary Josephine' for the second year while GARY had 'Sister Mary Gemma, R.S.M.' for 1st grade. In September my Dad bought us our 1st black & white TV. We regularly watched "The Mickey Mouse Club." In later years I enjoyed "The Hardy Boys' mysteries." It was different watching the story unfold daily on TV as opposed to reading all of their adventure stories. One of the things that TV taught me was language skills, instead of repeating dictionary words like 'Sister Mary Josephine' had my Mother do with me every school night during 1st grade.

3rd grade was very 'remarkable.'

We learned under the tutelage of our first lay teacher. [Nancy Kaufman's Mother was our second lay teacher for three months in a later grade.]

In 3rd grade I broke my left collarbone (I wrote right handed). Gary and I were playing football in our back yard. Yes, we were tackling each other even though that was against my Father's rules. I had my arm in a sling for six weeks. The day after the accident we were to elect class officers for the first time. Because I was absent they delayed the vote. 'JoAnn' became President and I was the honorary Vice-President. I don't remember who was Secretary and who was Treasurer.

In early December I accepted the chance to become "the youngest altar boy." I had to memorize all the Latin responses. The dialogue of prayers at the beginning of Mass was the hardest to pronounce correctly. On Monday March 19th (the Feast of St. Joseph) I served the 7 am Mass. My Dad regularly attended that Mass. 'Mike Farnsworth' (4th grade) served the 8 am School Children's Mass (the Mass that my Mom regularly attended). ['Mike' went on to become the Captain of the Safety Patrol in the 8th grade; then he attended Seminary for two or three years in Wisconsin.]

For Christmas Dad drove our lay teacher to her hometown of Cheboygan (22 miles SE of the Mackinaw Bridge). With this Bridge we no longer had to take the car ferry. Then we drove on to Iron Mountain for my only 'Iron Mountain Christmas.' Grandpa put an unwrapped saw and hammer under the tree for Christmas morning. Gary and I each received our own set.

After my 8th birthday (2nd grade) I phoned 'Fran VanderKolk' about becoming a Cub Scout. She said her den of eight was full. In September of 1955 my Mother became "Den Mother" of Den 2. It became a loving four year commitment every Monday after school until Gary joined the Boy Scouts at age 11. Yes, 'Mr. Al Schinderle,' was our 1st Scoutmaster in this his 2nd time of serving.

4th grade art:

The highlight of this academic year was our make-believe movie screen, a scroll of Bible characters and Bible encounters. My contribution to this Biblical scroll was a picture of 'Cain.' My assigned buddy and I drew and colored Cain's vegetables. Then we did not like our picture so we blackened everything. SIN once again had entered Plant Earth.

I wonder what pictures 'Kathy' drew and colored. [She graduated from 'Ferris'; then after 25 years teaching typing in Bellaire she entered the convent and became 'Sister Kathlyn Lange.']

5ᵗʰ grade: Funeral Masses and ice hockey

Three of our girls (JoAnn, Emalee, and Jane Westley) played the piano first, then graduated to the church organ. They alternated the 8 am High Mass and the occasional funerals. After each funeral Mass each of us four boys received $5.00 – enough to buy a pagan baby from the mission field. I name my first such ransom, 'John Michael,' not 'Ronald, Ronald, Ronald.'

During Christmas vacation the weather was perfect for ice hockey. We found a secluded pond on the east side of the Muskegon River. We crossed the river on the old railroad bed. That was before the dam was removed. I had tube skates and was a poor skater. Therefore, I was one of the two goalies. Our fun ended when a six inch snow storm covered our mystery spot. That was the only winter we used that location to skate.

I began 6ᵗʰ grade at age 11.

By now my Dad had challenged me to a one year competition of who would receive Holy Communion the most. If I slept in on Saturday morning, Dad would cut into my lead. He also narrowed the gap considerably during summer vacation. I won the challenge by about "75 Holy Communions." He taught me the value of Daily Mass.

During the summer preceding 6ᵗʰ grade my Dad built a box hockey ('box-socky') game. It had a wooden bottom, three compartments, a goalie hole at each end, and two holes in both of the middle dividers. Gary and I used broom stick handles cut about 39 inches long. We had some memorable games! The first time it was in action outside of our basement the Boy Scouts at St. Mary's had a Christmas tournament. I met and defeated 'Larry

Westley' in the finals. The following year Gary was a Boy Scout and we again had a tournament. This time I had to be a humble, gracious loser as Gary defeated me in the 2nd round.

In the 6th grade we boys were offered positions in the Safety Patrol captained by 'Van Westley.' In the 7th grade 'Michael Farnsworth' was the Captain, and in the 8th grade I was elected 'Captain.' No one won a trip to Washington, D.C., but 'Van Westley' was the most deserving.

It was in the 6th grade that we had our only 11-man tackle football team. We changed in and out of our uniforms in the Boy Scout room in the basement of St. Mary's School. 'Van Westley' was our QB (quarterback) and most talented player. In high school he also was the starting QB for the JVs and then the Varsity.

7th grade: Freedom and spreading my wings!

Our class was divided for the 1st time: half went with the 15 or 16 **8th graders** and half helped the 6th graders (Gary, Rebecca, and Ann Marie included). 'Sister Mary Caroline, R.S.M.' taught me and the Upper Grade. This was her 5th and last year as 'Principal.' We had two academic highlights: a Social Studies bee including all the 7th graders versus the 8th graders; and a debate – "Who was the greater President, George Washington or Abraham Lincoln?" My Dad coached our 7th grade Team for 'Honest Abe.' I was the 3rd of our five speakers for 'Abraham Lincoln.'

Athletically, we had our only basketball team. 'Joe Brissette' was our center (8th grade). I was one of our forwards and averaged two points a game plus rebounds. 'Mike Horrigan' and 'Philip Busch' were our two shooting guards (6th grade). We lost to St.

Peter's Lutheran three times. In the playoffs we were trounced by "Trufant."

8th grade: creativity, diversity, and Fun!!

'Sister Mary Ralph, R.S.M.' ('Sister Eleanor Marie' – post Vatican II) was very spontaneous and thorough as a Teacher / Principal. We even had three issues of a school newspaper.

It was 1960 and we held a Presidential Debate, "Kennedy vs. Nixon." Each team had five speakers. 'Sister' invited the 7th graders to listen thereby expanding our audience. We spoke in the school basement.

For 'All Saints Day' (November 1st) we had "a class box social" with me as the auctioneer. David Waddell asked for JoAnn's box to be sold first. Of course he was the highest bidder. [Years later his Mother served on the Big Rapids City Commission.] Nancy Currie's box went to Donald Foust at the highest price of any of the boxes. I ended up buying Arlene Johnson's box. [Her Dad succeeded my Dad as Scoutmaster for St. Mary's Troop 117.]

During the winter months 'Sister' had us "square dancing" in the basement / cafeteria of the school. We did not have an expected basketball team, but we did publish a school newspaper. I was the reporter that interviewed Joseph Spedowski.

In the spring 'Sister' oversaw Jim Knapp and I choosing our softball teams from the 7th and 8th grade boys. He had Philip Busch (2nd baseman and heavy hitter) and Philip Holman, the last man chosen. I traded one of my players to get 'the two Philips.' My Brother Gary was our 5th hitter after me; his ground rule double (hit the tree leaves) and scored me from 2nd base to tie the score in Game One, a suspended game with two outs in the bottom of the 3rd inning, our last inning. We kept these teams and I was the winner in all three, but it was suspenseful in the 1st game. The 7th and 8th grade girls also had two teams with 'lopsided final scores.'

In April 1961 I took and passed the entrance exam for St. Joseph's Seminary at 600 Burton Street in Grand Rapids, MI. Father Quaderer (later Monsignor Quaderer) took me to the Orientation / Field Day at St. Joe's in May.

As a Boy Scout I earned the rank of "Life Scout" with 10+ merit badges. Ben VanderKolk became our troop's "Eagle Scout" with 21 merit badges and a Community Service Project. He went on to become a dentist.

For 'Fire Safety Day' I went with the two firemen who had the churches. We swapped St. Mary's Church for St. Peter's School. Our 1st visit was "the 7th Day Adventist Church and School on Rose Avenue," two blocks from St. Mary's.

'Sister' took us on a Science Field trip, walking four blocks to visit "The Water Filtration Plant." We celebrated the end of the school year with a picnic / softball game at School Section Lake umpired by 'Sister.' We all graduated as "Winners."

IN THE KITCHEN:

My Mother was a fabulous cook. Dad grew the tomatoes and Mom fixed the noon BLTs (Bacon, lettuce, tomato sandwiches with or without the mayo, toasted or plain white bread). After lunch Dad would prop-up the green recliner and take a "20 minute nap." He ate lunch at home often.

My Mother was a fabulous cook. My Brother Gary's favorite meal was spaghetti with "many, many meatballs." It was as good as the native Italian pasta I ate in Italy.

My Mother was a fabulous cook. One night as an adult I ate five hard-shell tacos with all the trimmings and medium hot sauce. Growing up I favored Mom's pork chops, baked potatoes with sour cream, and specially seasoned sauce on the pork chops.

My Dad was usually home from work by 5:30-5:45. He always gave my Mother a BIG HUG and a KISS in the kitchen. Mom did not wear red lipstick or go to the nail parlor for her fingers. In her later years she went to a podiatrist to get her toe nails clipped.

WITHIN FOUR BLOCKS FROM HOME:

Eric D. Williams, Big Rapids City Attorney since September 1986, has his office on the SE corner of North State Street and E. Grand Traverse. He schedules evenings and Saturday appointments (something my Dad did not do). In addition to his Catholic morality and raising his family he is 'a dominant' competitive chess player.

Bowers Restaurant was on the NE corner of this interchange. Wayne & Alma Wortley were the owners of this north-end restaurant. They hosted 'the Big Rapids Rotary Club' every Monday from 6:00-7:30 pm for several years.

Along the east side of North State Street in the 600 block there was Bowers, Andrew's Photography, State Street Hardware, and Grunst Bros. Sporting Goods and Party Supplies.

Along the west side of North State in the 600 block there was a grocery store, Liberty Dairy, and a barber shop. I did get a few haircuts there, but normally my Dad cut my hair. We got hand-dipped ice cream cones at Liberty Dairy. John Emmons delivered milk by quart glass bottles to our back (not fenced in) Patio, two bottles per delivery from Emmons Dairy.

Question: What makes some Writings "SO SPECIAL"?

Answer: The secret that distinguishes professional writing from that of "the average Joe" is given us by KODAK: *"The genius is in the details."*

My Parents

My Mother, 'Kathleen' – Irish form of Catherine, is a native of Graceville, Minnesota. Her Catholic Confirmation name is 'Rose of Lima.' Her father was a government dentist who retired at age 65 and lived another 31 years in retirement. My father grew up in Iron Mountain, a city 100 miles north of Green Bay, Wisconsin. 'Albin' was the valedictorian of his high school class and passed the Michigan "Bar Exam" following his junior year at the University of Michigan Law School. His heart murmur kept him out of active duty during World War II. Instead he taught riveting at the Willow Run Bomber Plant. (This is probably where he developed 'deafness' in his left ear.)

My parents met at the "U of M" Catholic Chapel where my Dad served as janitor for 'Monsignor Allen J. Babcock.' Years later 'Bishop Babcock' made my appointment to study in Rome, making this appointment on his deathbed. My Mother earned a degree in "Library Science." They married on 23 October 1944 in St. Cloud, MN. Travel by train was BIG then.

Trusting God for children

Until I was conceived in May 1946 my parents relied on Faith that they would have children even though my Mother had one ovary removed before the Sacrament of Matrimony. My Mother carried me in her womb for the full nine months and had a natural child birth with me and with my Brother Gary (20 months younger – one grade difference in school). We never did get the baby sister our family prayed for when I was age 7 to 9. We recited the family rosary every evening on our knees for that intention.

A quick description of my Brother Gary

Gary began 1st grade when I began 2nd grade. He was less-baseball oriented than I, preferring hunting and fishing, high school and college tennis, and golf. He also was interested in auto mechanics and raced a car at the Cadillac fairgrounds. His personality is people-centered and practical. It served him well as a (high stress) salesman for 30 years at Xerox. He also was blessed with good judgment and a staunch Catholic morality.

Upon graduation from FERRIS his military status had him ticketed for Vietnam after he went through basic training. After a brief "good-bye" at Home he reported back to his Army base. Thanks to prayer his destination was changed to Bamberg, West Germany. It was there that he married 'Sue Ann,' his College sweetheart. In June 2011 they celebrated their 40th Wedding

Anniversary. He has one daughter, named 'Kristy.' I know he loves me.

My high school was at St. Joseph's
Seminary in Grand Rapids, MI.
Here I lived: schooling, sports, and Daily Prayer.

We began with "89 freshmen" (Sections A and B) and were joined by basketball star forward, 'Thomas D.,' as sophomores. Only one of us (not me) was ordained a Deacon. He ended up married to a classmate's sister, raised two sons, and worked for USPS.

"Driver's Ed" in Big Rapids

The summer following my 16th birthday I studied six weeks of bookwork and in-car driving. On my 1st day of driving 'Gus Southworth' or 'Howard Bale,' my instructor, had me drive one block north from Riverview School and then turn right. The results: I looked at my feet the first block; then I turned 150 degrees instead of a '120' and ended up on the grass. As you can tell this was my 1st attempt ever behind the wheel. After that my driving skills improved rapidly.

At the successful completion of the bookwork and the on-road driving my Dad wisely had me 'parallel park' using four stick poles on the street where my neighbor's driveway intersected. This alerted them to be careful backing out of their driveway! I was not allowed to apply for my regular driver's license until after Easter, at age 17.

I last drove a car in 1985. Because of the medicines I was / am on, it is no longer safe for me to drive. My night vision is defective also. My last license plate read: Michigan ATY 421.

Swimming

At age 13 I earned the Boy Scout 'swimming merit badge' as well as completing a mile swim. My Mother sewed my 'mile swim patch' on my swimsuit. This took place over a two week span at Camp Shawandosee (near Muskegon).

In October 2011 I joined three others for my 1st three month swim pass at The Holiday Inn in Big Rapids We each paid $30 = $120 for this privilege. One of the swimmers is 'a man born blind.' He needed assistance locating the Dial-A-Ride city bus from inside the lobby at the Holiday Inn during the winter season when it was too cold to wait alone outside the building.

In March 2013 we lost this privilege as new owners did not want to pay the needed insurance to keep the pool open to the general public. Since April 2014 two of us have been allowed to swim one day a week for $5 per person at the Super 8 Motel. They allow two of us because 'Doug' is visually impaired.

The Charles Fairman Community Pool

It was built in 1974-1975. The Health Department closed the old pool, the dammed up Mitchell Creek Pool. I learned to swim in that old pool. We had sandy wood change rooms, dormitory style then, one for the boys and one for the girls. We checked our clothes in numbered metal baskets and 'a checker' recorded our number for safe keeping.

The last item the new pool required was an emergency phone. They got one in two hours, blue in color – as Ms. Patricia Horan requested. I received this information in a phone interview with

Ms. Patricia Horan, who expected to be in charge of THE POOL for her 57th summer in 2012. Her philosophy / theology of life: "Good morning, God. Walk with me this new day."

Swede Hill Park

My morning kindergarten teacher at Hillcrest was Mrs. Miller. She was honored with a plaque at 'Swede Hill Park,' just north of the Canoe Livery on the east side of the Muskegon River. The afternoon of this 1999 dedication 'Hayworth Components' in the Industrial Park (which my Dad had City Attorney power over when the Industrial Park was created) was open for public visitation. My Mother and I toured 'Hayworth' before attending the short dedication of 'Swede Hill Park' in the late afternoon. In September 2010 the city retired Hillcrest School.

What are my "3" favorite movies?

'Gary Alber' and his wife 'Jan' invited me to be their guest on a Friday night at the Big Rapids Cinema to watch SEABISCUIT, a famous racehorse. Yes, I have enjoyed 'the Kentucky Derbe' on the 1st Saturday of May, 'the Preakness' two weeks later, and 'the Belmont Stakes' three weeks later. This is horse racing's TRIPLE CROWN, run by three-year-old horses.

My 2nd choice is RUDY, a story of an unlikely football player at Notre Dame. 'Rudy Schinderle' is my Grandpa. 'Rudy York,' a powerful HR (home run) hitter for the Detroit Tigers, was my Uncle Jake's favorite baseball player. My Niece Kristy graduated from Notre Dame with a Business & Finance degree (after spending the first two years with all women students at St. Mary's).

My 3rd choice is the baseball fantasy, FIELD OF DREAMS. All three of these movies are "Sports Genre." I would enjoy having a copy of any or all of these three movies. For me they are all CLASSICS. (I do not watch a lot of movies.)

Earning a living:

My Grandpa 'Rudy Schinderle' worked at "the Ford Motor Plant in Kingsford," a town connected to Iron Mountain. At 9:00 pm their whistle blew (CT – Central Time) for one minute. 90 days before his retirement the Plant closed down, and there was no retirement benefits. "Grandpa" started his own business in his basement at home, namely, sharpening saws and lawn mower blades on push lawn mowers, etc. He continued to buy Ford automobiles. When he died in 1962 he was driving a black Ford and my Dad inherited it. Dad donated it to 'the Sisters of Mercy, R.S.M.' who taught at St. Mary's Grade School, and one of the Sisters took "Driver's Ed" to be able to drive it.

Triangle Auto Sales

Beginning in 1917 in Big Rapids 'Triangle Auto Sales' was the dealership for Ford, Mercury, Lincoln. Both my Parents were born in 1920. As long as I can remember it was located at the NW corner of South State Street and Morrison. 'Burger King' is on the SW corner of that intersection. Growing up I recall that 'Robert Horan, Sr.' owned it. After his death it passed on to his son, 'Robert Horan, Jr.' (My Dad was "Scoutmaster" for 'Bob, Jr.' growing up.)

'Robert Horan III' played CF (centerfield) and I played SS (shortstop) in slo-pitch the one summer that Big Rapids had a Church Softball League. St. Mary's came in 1st place.

WWW = Wolverine World Wide

At one time 'WWW' operated two factories in Big Rapids to make shoes and boots. They opened a retail store in town, 'The Little Red Shoe House' – at the NE corner of North State and E. Waterloo. Their main store was in Rockford (on US-131 about 40 miles south). When the demand for their shoes diminished, they closed their plant on North Michigan Avenue (the current location of 'Big Rapids Public Safety'). Since "2000" they have fulfilled large military contracts for boots at their 'Baldwin Avenue' site (east of the Muskegon River and east of North State Street). Across from 'Big Rapids Public Safety' is The Big Rapids Middle School for grades 6th, 7th, and 8th. Originally, this was the site for the local ice skating rink. I learned to skate there using "Tube skates." Soon thereafter I began my newspaper business with "the Pioneer." Now I was started "in the Marketplace."

The richest man in Big Rapids was 'Top Taggert,' the man who earned his fortune in the Austin Gas Field. He made "FERRIS" a "GO" from the ashes of the fire of the early 1950s. The Ferris State University football field is named in his honor, 'Top Taggert Field.' Mr. Taggert donated the land for St. Paul's Catholic Chapel at 1 Damascus Road. My father was the lawyer that represented St. Mary's Parish when the students' need for a Building came to reality. The Taggert House is located at the NW corner of Maple

Street and N. Stewart (just east of the old Post Office). For a time it was "a Bed-n-Breakfast." That ended when a small electrical fire started in the attic. The Fire Department was able to put that fire out in a hurry and save the structure.

Big Rapids Restaurants

I prefer these "3" special restaurants in 2014. "The Rock Café" at Ferris State University ($9.25 for all you can eat for lunch or supper). "Arby's" on the east side of the Muskegon River (next to New Journey Clubhouse). And "Applebee's" (newly remodeled) on Perry Avenue. My all-time favorite, "Ponderosa Steakhouse in Big Rapids," closed in the early summer of 2011.

I remember my Dad's 66th birthday celebration, 26 July 1986. We went to "Ponderosa Steakhouse" and as we were arriving 'Joe and Marigrace Baldwin' were leaving. For my 66th birthday I went to "Ponderosa Steakhouse in Mt. Pleasant, MI." In Big Rapids my favorite meal was "Sirloin Tips with French fries and salad bar." In Mt. Pleasant I had "Senior Buffet."

Growing up in Big Rapids we seldom went out to eat in Big Rapids as a family of four. On birthdays MOM cooked and we had cake and ice cream. In high school seminary we had soda pop and cake, serving eight students.

On Wednesday 2 January 2013 my retired 'Chief Master Sergeant Mark S. Brejcha' treated me to breakfast at "Wild Rose Café' next to Currie's BP gas station on the east side of town. Then in the process of doing errands he stopped to show me the World War I memorial at "FERRIS." He pointed out two 'Ferris Institute' students that had names "in memorial of." These two students are the basis of our airport name, "Roben-Hood Airport" located north of the city.

My Mother, now age 93, lives at an Assisted Living Home in Big Rapids.

> "When we believe in God's plan for us, that
> very age is the perfect age to be."
> (These words are taken from a favorite birthday
> card from my Brother Gary and his wife.)

Our neighborhood children:

Our one block went from Marion Avenue (east), Pere Marquette Street (north), Rose Avenue (west) and W. Waterloo Street (south). There were ten of us: Ronald, Gary, Roger, David, Lois, Geraldine, Pam, Judy, Patricia, and Marvin (nicknamed 'Fugi'). We played croquet in two different sized lots; softball, kickball, and "Red Rover, Red Rover, send _____ right over" in our backyard; hide-and-go seek / Free the Slaves – in two other backyards; "enee, eine, over" before our house and garage became united through remodeling; capture the flag – east of our North / South alley.

Adulthood

Later in life 'Roger' brought his four-year-old son to visit me one summer afternoon. 'Judy' married the Circuit Court Judge. 'Patricia' died at a young age in an out-of-state car accident. 'Fugi' excelled in Slo-pitch softball. My Brother worked diligently "30 years" for Xerox; then retired with a 1999 home in Florida on two golf courses and a house at Canadian Lakes in Michigan on another golf course. In 2013 and 2014 he and his partner won 'the Gold Medal' in pickleball in the SE U.S.A. Regionals in Naples, Florida (double elimination against 15-16 teams).

I put Christ 1st in my life.
I went where the Bible told me, "GO."

I, Ronald, am a powerful man of Heaven!

2ND TIMOTHY 1:7 – KJV. "For God has not given us the spirit of fear; but of power, and of love, and of a sound mind."

From: Walt & Sophie Novak, 'Catholic Charismatic Leaders,' who retired in Ocala, Florida.

(Ron), "God needs you right where you are."

Weddings:

'Elijah and Caroline': "May this be a Road to generations – AMEN."

Praise God cheerfully – 1, 5-31-2014

What was the 1ˢᵗ musical instrument invented on Earth?

GENESIS 4:21 – KJV. "And his brother's name was Jubal: he was the father of all such as handle the harp and organ."

GENESIS 4:21 – The MESSAGE. "His brother's name was Jubal, the ancestor of all who play the lyre and flute."

PSALMS 33:2-3. [KJV]. "Praise the LORD with harp: sing unto him with the psaltery and an instrument of ten strings. (3) Sing unto him a new song; play skilfully with a loud noise."

PSALMS 34:1 – KJV. "I will bless the LORD at all times: his praise shall continually be in my mouth."

PSALMS 95:1 – KJV. "O come, let us sing unto the LORD: let us make a joyful noise to the rock of our salvation."

PSALMS 96:1-2. [KJV]. "O sing unto the LORD a new song: sing unto the LORD, all the earth. (2) Sing unto the LORD, bless his name; shew forth his salvation from day to day."

PSALMS 98:1 – KJV. "O sing unto the LORD a new song; for he hath done marvellous things: his right hand, and his holy arm, hath gotten him the victory."

PSALMS 100:1-2. [KJV]. "Make a joyful noise unto the LORD, all ye lands. (2) Serve the LORD with gladness: come before his presence with singing."

Prophecy from African-American Co-Pastor Sheron Strong:

"Get ready for a sudden and necessary change in your life! ... God is doing some housekeeping and he's getting rid of junk! ... ... You'll be so happy at what He replaces the junk with! Get ready for the new!!>>>."

The wealthiest place on Earth is the cemetery. Why is that the truth? According to 'Myles Munroe' that is where the wealth of 'Untapped Potential' rests.

Success is discovering your God-given abilities and learning how to use them skillfully and productively.

'A TESTIMONY' showcases the life of the righteous and gives God the glory. The role model who is honest and honorable leaves a legacy of God, working with men and women ☺ + ☺.

"Let God bless you always."

PSALMS 66:16 – KJV. "Come and hear, all ye that fear God, and I will declare what he hath done for my soul."

"Available am I"

I told that to God as early as the 6th grade when I decided I wanted to be a Catholic priest.

I told that to God on Saturday 18 December 1971 in St. Peter's Basilica (Vatican City State) as I became "born-again" and made my 1ˢᵗ Adult Profession of Faith.

I told that to God in August 1977 when I packed all my possessions into my car for the "90 mile drive" east to Bay City with two part-time jobs and no housing. I left my Parents' house like 'Abram & Sarai' as they left their city of Ur.

> I told that to God in May 2013 when I completed
> "Each New Day Facing Life with …"
> "Pray and do not give up." This is the
> correct meaning of 'Courage.'

Do you believe "Prayer is greater than money"? Why? "Because Prayer brings God's favor." Do not stop! You push, push, push until you win through God's help and favor. Pray without ceasing. When circumstances slow me down, I must trust God to carry me through the problem; prepare me for the bigger vision; and expect a whole new level of living and loving. I now live in the present one day at a time; no longer expecting and living for yesterday to repeat itself in today. This is the meaning of being healed of "Chronic Depression and Schizophrenia." By not giving up and by giving all the honor, glory, and praise to God above: this is 'Healing.'

BOOK – FOOD

"It matters a good deal that your book-food should be strong meat. We are what we think about. Think about trivial things or weak things and somehow one loses fibre and becomes flabby of spirit." (Rev. Billy Graham's wife, 'Ruth Bell Graham,' offers this pearl from 'Amy Carmichael' in her "1989 Desk Calendar" – WORD & WISDOM, June 25th.)

"Do I, do you, GIVE GOD THANKSGIVING before and after we enter the daily business world?" My Father 'Albin' did.

"As champion I'll play" (September 1972)

My Dad, nicknamed 'Smiley,' took up golf in 1967 saying he wanted to do something meaningful with me! It was the year after I had taken up this sport with such enthusiasm. Even though he was hit with an errant golf shot in 1966 while I was enjoying the course with him at 'Lake Waconia' (Minnesota), he was not timid nor afraid.

The Gospel, when lived out in the routine and the not so routine of each day / night, is "cutting edge technology" for the Christian attuned to the still small voice of the Holy Spirit or the cry of the lukewarm searching for answers to the Why, When, Where, How (of Life).

A Biblical Challenge:

Does Christ Jesus really, really know me even though I have been in Church (preparing to be the Bride of Christ at the Marriage Feast of the Lamb) all my life? This may seem like a stupid question, but for many 'so-called Christians' it means HEAVEN or HELL. (Do not be deceived: Satan is really real.) Not everyone who says "Lord, Lord" will enter heaven. GOD desires a deep, on-going, intimate relationship with each of us. He created each of us in His own image and likeness (male and female) to know, love, and serve Him.

The longest I ever lived away from Big Rapids was 7+ years (August 1977 to December 1984). I found an upstairs apartment located halfway between the north and south campuses of the Bay City All Saints Cougars and paid $110 rent to two different owners before the 3rd owner raised my rent to $125 a month beginning in November 1984. It was at this point in time that my Dad stepped in and invited me to become his "legal assistant in training." All my friends said that this was the opportunity of a lifetime.

Up to then I was on minimal funds as the church secretary at "House of Praise," a Pentecostal church on the west side of Bay City where I served capably for Pastor Ross Lakes (an Indiana native). At age 64 my father was "acutely aware, near semi-retirement, and needed his 1st born to be his hands and feet." As the Big Rapids city attorney he practiced law at 117 ½ South Michigan Avenue. This was two blocks south of City Hall. City Commission meetings were on the 1st and 3rd Mondays of each month, beginning at 7:30 pm. The Mecosta County Courthouse was 2 ½ blocks SE of his upstairs office.

His pet phrase for me was: "I read you like a book. I read you like a book."

"As we mature and grow older we constantly transition from the familiar to the new unknown." (Bud Ozar). This is helpful knowledge for me as I shape this autobiography without delusions.

'Dawn' agrees: [Beautiful]

I urge you: Stand strong in the Foundation
of your Faith. (EPHESIANS 6:10-20)
I HAVE BEEN.

That means spending lots of time exploring the Love of God.

How many of you would hesitate to defend in prayer … a drunk … a pauper … a congressman … a revolutionary Mormon … or the famous Jehovah Witness twins (ages 34 and 32)? Honestly, Ronald!! Are you kidding us? My church, 'Radical Impact Ministries,' promotes Prayer for these people. They have Destinies and days fashioned for them by God. (PSALMS 139)

Humorous: The not so wise fool named 'Sososo' lays up a kilogram (2.2 pounds) or a ton of gold. The stupid fool named 'Wind-sorry' lays up food for his Treasure. They are not rich towards God.

Zero. Empty? Hollow? Forgotten? Left for dead like Paul outside one city unmentionable. Some people have a 3:13 pm CDT landing in Chicago, the Windy City, home of 'the Sox' and nine miles north "the Cubs."

SALVATION: "Learn. Listen. Understand."

I think 'Moses, Moses' remembered for a lifetime where his "burning bush" was located.

"You are blessed indeed, mr. ron"

GOD commanded us to use things and love people. Give me a $^\wedge$5.

Continue to pray and study the Word of God, the Bible.

1ST CORINTHIANS 16:13 – The MESSAGE. "Keep your eyes open, hold tight to your convictions, give it all you've got."

"God has won the day again." (Pastor Joe)

Amen = so be it.

I followed Co-Pastor Sheron Strong's prophecy and housecleaned my apartment. Dawn's reaction: "I'm impressed."

With Abba, Jesus, and the Holy Spirit I aim to live each new day with Faith, Courage, and Optimism. This is the essence of "FACING LIFE ..."

My own proof: "God exists."

First of all, I examine the awesome beauty of nature: the sunrise and the sunset; the phenomenon called a half rainbow or full rainbow, and the rare double rainbow or the triple sunset rainbow using the colors orange, gray, and white. Of course, there is the contrast between the majestic mountain peaks and the mountain lake in the valley below. The formation of clouds as the sun shines and the blue sky is also glorious.

Secondly, what has man helped create? Most notable and noticeable is the layout of golf courses, especially the championship professional golf courses spread out among the countries of the world. Here again "the Man upstairs" paints the friendly skies.

Thirdly, what about the conception of each new human being? Then there is the delivery after he / she is carried to term. Watch the loving mother's hands and arms as she cradles her newborn infant. All former pains of child bearing are forgotten as the newborn's birth is celebrated.

Fourthly, consider the last breaths and facial expressions as I tell him to "Look at the Light" or "Go for the Light."

Fifthly, 'the Good Book' relates the story of the miracle of the ram caught in the thicket as 'Father Abraham' was about ready to sacrifice his son, 'Isaac,' on the altar at Mt. Moriah.

It is so easy to 'Praise God cheerfully' on birthdays because it is then that we celebrate and thank God for one more year of life! We also anticipate the newness that God's grace and mercy will provide in the days ahead. It is all accomplished by His great LOVE.

Speaking of "More birthdays"

"You've always been a good man, But when it comes to having a big heart, a generous nature, and a ready word of encouragement – you just seem to get better and better! (In 2011), Have a Happy 64th Birthday, Ron." Ron – the perfect card from me to you. Thanks for always being there. Your Friend, Mark (Brejcha).

What am I thirsty for?
For God's answers to our questions!

For a two-year-old: information of the mind profits much

For the toddler: Knowledge + energy + Love

1ST CORINTHIANS 10:13 – KJV. "There hath no temptation taken you but such as is common to man: but God is faithful, who will not suffer you to be tempted above that ye are able; but will with the temptation also make a way to escape, that ye may be able to bear it."

1ST CORINTHIANS 10:13 – The MESSAGE. "No test or temptation that comes your way is beyond the course of what others have had to face. All you need to remember is that God will never let you down; he'll never let you be pushed past your limit; he'll always be there to help you come through it."

In Italy 'Babo Natale' is "Father Christmas."
In South Africa 'Baba' is "God the Father."

Recognize the thirst for power in the work place or in the marketplace. It is here that the thirst for advancement, promotion is a driving force. It helps to say "Thanks, God" before you leave Home and upon arriving at Home.

I 'Praise God cheerfully' for the dimple on my face just above my chin. My Grandpa Schinderle's father migrated to the U.S.A. around 1890 A.D. His family DNA produced a dimple the size of a dot on his face where he shaved his chin. (Thus the name 'Chinderle' in Austria.) My Dad 'Albin,' my Brother 'Gary' and I have this dimple. I call it a mark of honor and favor bestowed by God.

Q. Tell us a little more about your Dad's family background.

A. 'Joseph Arsenault' (Alsace-Lorraine) was Grandma Clara Schinderle's brother. He never married and he lived his whole life in Iron Mountain / Kingsford. He never own a car. He walked.

'Rudy & Clara' lived on the Italian North Side on the corner of Main + Aragon. 'Uncle Joe' lived on the other side of "the pit." He lived on the west side. "The pit" was divided into East and West by Highway US-2. The ski jumping bunny hill was on the east side of "the pit." 'Henry Jacob' was warned by his father. When he came home from ski jumping with a broken leg (literally), 'Rudy'

–true to his word- cut up Henry's skis and used it for kindling for his coal furnace.

I easily can 'Praise God cheerfully' for my military career. Because I was in the seminary (divinity student) I was classified as "4-D." That kept me out of the fury of the war in Vietnam. The year they had the draft lottery my birthday February 22nd received a "265-270" number. I entered this draft lottery in 1972 but they drafted very few people that year. "I praise your holy name, dear Yahweh."

When you live entirely for God and His Kingdom as MATTHEW 6:33 and LUKE 12:31 command, GOD Jehovah protects and blesses you. That does not mean that you are spared UPs and DOWNs, but it does mean God is our 'Good Shepherd.'

My two weeks as a Chaplain's Assistant in 1970 in Baumholder, SW Germany, climaxed with the Catholic Chaplain taking us three Roman seminarians to 'the LIVE Passion Play' put on every ten years by the city residents of Oberammergau.

In 1971 in Stuttgart, Germany during my three week stay 'Chaplain Spietel' took me golfing all three Saturdays (my only golf in Europe). I also had my tennis racquet. It was there that I distributed Holy Communion on the Tongues for my only times I gave 'the Eucharist' in my lifetime.

It was at Stuttgart that I realized I must make an adult decision as to whether or not I would become a Catholic priest. As it turned out God made the permanent decision an easy one to choose. At Stuttgart the official Chaplains' Assistant (Catholic and Protestant) was an ex-seminarian. The one night 'Fr.' Bob Striegel from Iowa and I ate in the soldiers' mess hall with, I will call him, 'Thomas' he challenged my childhood dream: "Why should 'I' become a Catholic priest?" I prayed from that July through December 1971, asking God for "a sign." On 18 December 1971 in the front of St. Peter's Basilica the class ahead of mine became ordained as Priests. I stood in the bright sunlight under the dome of St. Peter's and told God I would do whatever He had in store for me the remainder of my life. Within a week I was back in Big Rapids with my Parents, suffering from the beginning of a nervous breakdown from STRESS, STRESS, and MORE STRESS. In April 1972 I met with 'Bishop Joseph Breitenbeck' in Grand Rapids and we decided I would not become a Catholic priest for the Grand Rapids diocese.

Amid the fluffy afternoon cumulus clouds the sun kept reappearing. It was an 80 degree June 2014 day in Big Rapids. It was not long before a fox squirrel and a lone robin graced my backyard. My neighbor across the balcony from me had said, "You look cheerful today."

I certainly do 'Praise God cheerfully' for allowing me to receive "the Baptism of the Holy Spirit" as a Catholic. I was introduced to the Catholic Charismatic Renewal during November / December 1971. I attended two Sunday afternoon gatherings (2-4 pm) with 'Fr.' Edward Scharfenberger from Brooklyn, N.Y. We met in the Building opposite the Gregorian University in the west side of 'the Piazza' in front of THE GREG.

Back in Big Rapids I attended a six week "Life in the Spirit Seminar," with my Mother driving the 12 miles to St. Philip Neri in Reed City. At that time I was skeptical of receiving "the Baptism of the Holy Spirit" and speaking in Tongues.

After moving to Bay City in August 1977 I began attending the Charismatic Prayer Group at St. Joseph's Parish in central Bay City. In the winter of 1979 I did receive "the Baptism of the Holy Spirit" without doubts or trepidation. My 1ˢᵗ word in Tongues came in a dream: "Thelmarretsin" - "I want the sea of cleansing."

After returning to Big Rapids from Bay City in November 1984 I worked six month in my Dad's Law Office. During the time in June 1985 that my Parents moved my Mother's Dad (Dr. Aloysius Trainor) from Waconia, Minnesota to Big Rapids I had to be hospitalized in Midland for … "schizoaffective, bipolar type." In October 1985 I had to be re-hospitalized in Midland. After I was released from this Psychiatric Health unit I was admitted to 'the Williamson Adult Foster Care Home' 2 ½ blocks from my Parents.

I then started to attend the end of the Thursday night Mass and the Charismatic Prayer Meeting that followed in St. Mary's Parish Room. Both my Parents attended the Mass and the Prayer Meeting. They never spoke in Tongues.

In September 2009 at Christ's Harvest Ministries aka Revival Christian Center 'Rev. Bryce Perry,' (a native of Calgary, Canada) preached and 'Arnie' led a prayer walk to the Maple Street Bridge in Big Rapids. It was there that I joined "the Artillery in God's Army." I prayed LOUD, LOUD, and LOUDER in Tongues. Ever since that day 'Tongues' has been a spiritual weapon for me to use for God. It enhances the range of the Holy Spirit.

During 2013 'Aloma Jean Grein' taught on how to easily "Speak in Tongues." This took place while she was attending 'Radical Impact Ministries' Sunday Worship at Pepper's Café and Deli.

Her technique: begin speaking the notes of the musical scale (Do, re, mi, fa, sol, la, ti, do). Soon you will be speaking in your 'God-language.' This technique increased my vocabulary.

What is 'meekness'?

Eugene H. Peterson in The MESSAGE describes 'Meekness' as one of the beatitudes in MATTHEW 5:5. "You're blessed when you're content with just who you are – no more, no less. That's the moment you find yourselves proud owners of everything that can't be bought."

The fruits of the Holy Spirit

GALATIANS 5:22-23. [KJV]. "But the fruit of the Spirit is love, joy, peace, longsuffering, gentleness, goodness, faith, (23) Meekness, temperance: against such there is no law."

GALATIANS 5:22-23. [The MESSAGE]. "But what happens when we live God's way? He brings gifts into our lives, much the same way that fruit appears in an orchard – things like affection for others, exuberance about life, serenity. We develop a willingness to stick with things, a sense of compassion in the heart, and a conviction that a basic holiness permeates things and people. We find ourselves involved in loyal commitments, not needing to force our way in life, able to marshal and direct our energies wisely."

I 'Praise God cheerfully' for Reed City Missionary in Nicaragua 'Jack Nehmer.' He shared with me his criterion to evaluate autobiographies: "How is Scripture applied in the author's life and in encouraging his / her readers' lives"?

What is the purpose of writing an autobiography? Co-Pastor Sheron Strong encourages: "God wants you to tell your story and save someone else's Life."

THE PRAYER OF JABEZ is a book-commentary on Jabez's Prayer as recorded in 1ST CHRONICLES 4:9-10. I am praying for the God of Israel to bless me indeed. "Indeed" means 'in ways I can see and touch.' Therefore, it is something tangible. I am also praying that He expand and extend my territory. Also that He keeps me from evil and from causing pain to any person that reads or listens to my writings.

Today's challenge: *Compliment "3" people meaningfully,* remembering that flattery gets you nowhere.

Are you missing something or someone today? A gospel suggestion: *"Call on Him."* JESUS would love to hang out with you today, any day, or even every day!

Mental illness does not define me nor should it stop me from achieving my goals and dreams. In Jesus Mighty Name I am healed. I will continue to work with Doctors; I realize I must take a certain amount of meds. This is being realistic and not delusional.

I 'Praise God cheerfully' for my seven day stay (June 27 – July 3, 2013) at Mid Michigan Medical Center in Midland. I really needed a med change!!!! Three Doctors in Big Rapids were prescribing meds for me to take at different times, for different medical reasons. It got confusing for me.

Entering Midland I was taking 12 meds. Leaving Midland I had an increase in two, a reduction to half strength in one, and a discontinuation of two. Today I am taking the 10 meds with a reduction of one of the added strength meds because of negative side effects. I also needed a new weekly pill container that I refill every Wednesday evening. I take my meds at 9:30 am or earlier, 6 pm and 9:30 pm.

I have heard it said repeatedly: "Live one day at a time." To that I would add: "Don't rush it." HEBREWS 13:8 – Jesus says that He is the same yesterday, today, and tomorrow.

> Each day at Mid Michigan Medical Center was a new
> day, built on the previous day. That helped me learn
> the benefits of not dwelling on the past. My diagnosis
> entering 'Midland' was: "Schizophrenia disorder, bipolar
> type." Josh & Jean wrote on 'Radical Impact Ministries'
> get well card: "Praying For Healing (you will be Healed)."
> That is why I calmly write: "My schizophrenia is under
> control. My 2014 autobiography is not delusional. I thank
> God for guiding me to greater Clarity, coherence, and
> relevancy." O yes, THREE IN ONE, I worship Thee.
> "Blessings of Miracles Signs & Wonders
> over you –" (Bonita Bush)

GOD, my Loving Creator, You made me in Your own image for me to shine love and compassion to our end-time generation. I am a walking, living Bible (the Knight of the Word) to my peers who are "the saints" and "the ain'ts." As an evangelist, I believe my writings will touch the Lost and bring many to a personal relationship with Jesus of Nazareth, the Christ. He is our Savior, Lord, and King of kings. My writings are also intended to motivate the Church to be faithful to the Bible, (the written Word of God) and not to compromise with sin.

"Trusting GOD completely means having FAITH that he know what is BEST for your life." (Jannet: my youngest of three spiritual daughters).

With my renewed mind JESUS has plans 'through me' and not just 'for me."

"TILL THE NET IS FULL" – Harvest of souls

Thank God for our husbands!!!!!

"If you have a wonderful man, who helps balance your world .. who isn't perfect, but is perfect for you .. who works hard and would do anything for you .. that makes you laugh and drives you crazy .. who is your best friend, who you want to grow old with .. and who you are … thankful for everyday," Then ☺ let your friends and world know. You have a solid marriage. (From my Pastor's wife, 30 years married on November 24, 2014)

THE TEN COMMANDMENTS (in simplest form)

1. Put God first.
2. Worship the Lord.
3. Respect the Name of Jesus.
4. Go to church.
5. Honor your mom and dad.
6. Love is greater than hate.
7. Keep yourself pure.
8. Do not steal.

9. Tell the truth.
10. Be thankful.

As for 'Radical Impact Ministries' we are small but powerful. The Word of God brings change and newness to our city and the surrounding area. 'Job' in the [OT] established the principle that for your shame you get back double. Therefore, "Take courage."

A word of caution: Stop getting in people's faces with Negative words or comments to change their lives. Be a 1ST CORINTHIANS 13:4-7 action person in thought, words, deeds. Allow kindness, gentleness, and peace to take over.

As 'Michi' wrote in June 2013: "We are praying and thinking GREAT God things over you! The Holy Spirit is in and beside you Jesus has you in the palm of His Hand!"

Who determines my worth?

My approval rating is not based on people although many do encourage me to 'Go Deeper' with Abba Father, Jesus His divine and human Son, and my Advocate the Holy Spirit.

Let's grow in Hope!

Take one day at a time, have a plan, then turn the day over to God's care and trust Him for the outcome.

PHILIPPIANS 4:6a, 7b. [The MESSAGE]. "Don't fret or worry. Instead of worry, pray … it's wonderful what happens when Christ displaces worry at the center of your life."

Who determines my worth?

My Scriptural response to this question (as suggested by the Gideons) is "God's Greatness and Man's Weakness" (ISAIAH, chapter 40).

Scripture also says: SOW both in the am and
in the pm and God will determine how fruitful
you will be. (ECCLESIASTES 11:6)

"Father's Day" is / was the 3rd Sunday of June.

My earthly Father, 'Albin Joseph Schinderle,' lived a full, Godly life and died painlessly in his sleep on Saturday 6 September 1986 at home at the age of "66." I 'Praise God cheerfully' that he is / was a holy man. His unexpected death was a 1986 copy of Moses' death at age 120 because both spiritual leaders died when "eye was not dim, nor his natural force abated" (DEUTERONOMY 34:7). The MESSAGE describes their conditions: "His eyesight was sharp; he still walked with a spring in his step."

Having a Dad who loves you and who would do anything for you is a direct "generational blessing" from God. I returned his discipline with Loyalty. Together we go from birth into eternity and then on with God's Ultimate Provision whatever that will be.

1ST CORINTHIANS 13:13 – The MESSAGE. "But for right now, until that completeness, we have three things to do to lead us to that consummation: Trust steadily, hope unswervingly, love extravagantly. And the best of the three is love."

Cheerfulness is the beginning of Joy.

A leader for God – 1, 6-12-2014

Every leader starts as a follower. Whether that leader is a parent or a teacher or a person in sales education and experience make a difference. Even a baseball player must undergo some games in the minor leagues before he becomes a rookie learning from the veterans and his coaches and manager.

Truly, truly, parents qualify as leaders especially if they are beyond teenage years. Parents train their children to raise up grandchildren. New parents draw on their upbringing and learn much on the job. They also learn through meaningful questions.

In my situation my Parents brought me up to be a Catholic Priest and not the father of a biological family. Diapers and a lifetime of availability to my child or children did not appeal to me early on. In fact, it wasn't until age 30 in Bay City / Essexville that I had my 1st unchaperoned date.

"Transparency" is allowing others to look into my life as a glass window with gold etching on the inside of the glass. The etching is your clothing and jewelry if you are a woman of the Most High God.

What lesson did I really really learn from my Parents?

They taught me and brought me up to be a person of Prayer. Prayer of course takes on so many styles: from the most formal Prayer of all, the Mass, to individual conversations with THE THREE IN ONE.

As a seminarian preparing to preach the homily after the 1st reading and the Gospel passage 2ND TIMOTHY 2:15 – KJV describes my preparation. "Study to shew thyself approved unto God, a workman that needeth not to be ashamed, rightly dividing the word of truth."

DAILY PRAYER as an adult

HEBREWS 4:12 – KJV. "For the word of God is quick, and powerful, and sharper than any twoedged sword, piercing even to the dividing asunder of soul and spirit, and of the joints and marrow, and is a discerner of the thoughts and intents of the heart."

Becoming a person of Prayer: I grew from the rosary on my knees in the evening at home as a child, praying from age 7 to 9 for a baby sister, to daily Mass and Holy Communion (the Eucharist) as a youth, to being a charismatic filled with the Holy Spirit and speaking in tongues as an adult. Now that I am "the Knight of the Word" my training in Scripture helps others get closer to God.

What does Scripture do?

2ND TIMOTHY 3:16 – KJV. "All scripture is given by inspiration of God, and is profitable for doctrine, for reproof, for correction, for instruction in righteousness:"

If your mind can conceive it and your faith does not waver, then that mountain of ... inordinate expectation, stress, and fatigue can be cast into the sea. (MARK 11:23-24)

Perfectionism and self-esteem are two significant entities. They are not to be compared on the same scale as I did until at least 2008-2009. Back then 8.5 was my target for perfectionism and its opposite was 1.5 for self-esteem. Using the Gregorian University passing grade of "6.0" I now have lowered my perfectionism goal to '7' and my healthy self-esteem to a minimum of '6.' I told my Case Manager at CMHCM that my self-esteem now exceeds my consistent '7' for perfectionism. I am happy with that analysis.

Writers for God

"What can God do? If he did it before; He will do it again" (Pastor Spence). I would add: except for the Rainbow promise to Noah that He would never re-flood the whole Earth again.

PSALMS 126:5 – KJV. "They that sow in tears shall reap in joy."

"You have to have the faith to fail. That means 'have the faith to get up, run some more, take hits and come back.' Winning is FUN." (Pastor Joe: used by his vocal permission)

At Williamson's AFC Home I read and studied Phillip Keller's A SHEPHERD LOOKS AT PSALM 23. That gave me insight into how sheep live and how the meticulous master takes care of sheep. MATTHEW 25:31-46. I am a sheep and not a goat.

As a writer for God my Brother Gary encouraged: "Keep researching; keep re-searching."

PHILIPPIANS 4:4 – The MESSAGE. "Celebrate God all day, every day. I mean, revel in Him! Make it as clear as you can to all you meet that you're on their side, working with them and not against them." This is 'Integrity.'

Trust is "the response from My children that I desire most." "Waiting for Me to work, with your eyes on Me, is evidence that you really do trust Me." (Sarah Young – 40 Days with Jesus)

Sound moral character demands and requires 'Honesty & Loyalty.' Both Honesty and Loyalty are vital components of "Integrity."

As 'Sarah Young' prays: "Do not fear change, for I am making you *a new creation with old things passing away and new things continually on the horizon.*" Also, "the more you become *like Me,* the more you develop into the unique person I designed you to be."

From a baby on milk to a mature Christian on meat

HEBREWS 5:13-14. [KJV]. "For everyone that useth milk is unskilful in the word of righteousness: for he is a babe. (14) But strong meat belongeth to them that are of full age, even those who by reason of use have their senses exercised to discern both good and evil."

DEUTERONOMY 6:4-5. [The MESSAGE]. "Attention, Israel! GOD, our God! GOD the one and only! Love GOD, your God with your whole heart: love him with all that's in you, love him with all you've got!"

FAITH allows God to be God (whether or not we like the consequences). This requires our belief that He answers all our prayers either: (1) "Yes." (2) "Not quite yet." Or (3) "I have something better in mind for you."

PSALMS 19:14 – KJV. "Let the words of my mouth, and the meditation of my heart, be acceptable in thy sight, O LORD, my strength, and my redeemer." (This verse is a favorite of 'D.S. Asohan' of Malaysia.)

Let church walls / barriers come tumbling down as denominations and cultures come together to pray.

What is selfishness?

"Selfishness" wants another person to be available at my ever beckon call. It does not wait until the timing is more appropriate. Just for me, me, me. "Selfishness" is "I-centered."

Friendship
Fr. Max J. Frego (6-23-1928 to January 2010)
'<Maximilian Colby> Joseph.'

In 1962 his 1st assignment was to St. Mary's (Big Rapids) and St. Apollonia (Morley – 15 miles south). Fr. Quaderer (later Monsignor) was the Pastor in Big Rapids from 1957-1967.

Praying for 'Rev. Joseph N. Cottle' (based
on the prayer card of 'Terry Teykl')

Q. "What are the main distractions that every Pastor needs protection from?

A. "Busyness, unnecessary demands, fatigue, overcommitment, compromise, and doubt."

> ISAIAH 61:7 – The MESSAGE. "Because you
> got a double dose of trouble and more than your
> share of contempt, Your inheritance in the land
> will be doubled and your joy go on forever."
> "Keep praying and believing! … DON'T GIVE
> UP!!!!! (Co-Pastor Sheron Strong)
> 'Dawn,' you are certainly a leader (for God)
> in your family and in the work place.
> [I didn't let the devil get to me.]

> Sunshine, clouds, rain / snow: GOD creates them all.

When we pray for our shepherd, the Chief Shepherd gives our shepherd protection from "rumors, gossip, criticism, abuse, and ungratefulness." (Terry Teykl)

God created me as 'an eagle' to soar into the heavens. "When circumstances slow me down, I must trust God to carry me through the problem; prepare me for the bigger vision, and expect a whole new level of living and loving to come."

> "Never give up on something you can't go
> a day without thinking about."
> (Pastor Bryce Perry – then in Jacksonville, Florida)

> We have '168 hours' each week, and God holds us accountable.
> Become 'fruit inspectors.' As you examine the fruit
> you will discover and discern whether it is Good and
> Healthy for you. Have confidence in the Holy Spirit
> to assist you in this testing, selection process.

"Faith means 'taking one step at a time.' I must
totally trust the promise that GOD will do for
me what I could never do for myself."
"Profanity is pollution – word trash
that spoils the environment."

'Resurrection Sunday,' also known as "Easter" occurred on April 20, 2003 and 2014. It will occur again on April 20, 2025 and then not again until 2087 and 2098. My younger Grand Niece was born on April 20, 2004.

ROMANS 10:17 – KJV. "So then faith cometh by hearing, and hearing by the word of God."

I will join you in prayer for 'Pastor Joe' to have a thriving, flourishing ministry. His Master plan deserves our respect, devotion, and love. In other words, his Divine Appointments will steadily rise and his time will not be considered "inconsequential." Countless Souls will be won for the Kingdom. His sheep will be well taken care of.

Walk in what you know and keep learning!
You will be pleasantly surprised by what
God is doing for you and yours.
"Thank you for loving me, Jesus."

'Karl Linebaugh' (Chemical Bank Director) collects memorabilia!! He returned to me 'with interest' my 1955 collage with "Tom Ryan Cleaners" advertising on the reverse side. I was 8-years-old then, in the 3rd grade. "1955" was the city of Big Rapids' centennial year.

My assignment, our assignment, is to give God glory.

"The truth about me is always what God says! Not what I think or feel; not what others say, think or do. The truest thing about me is what God says!"

GOD labels me ... "Chosen, Forgiven, Restored, Redeemed, Valuable, a Masterpiece!!!" (Co-Pastor Sheron Strong – Chicago)

The Holy Spirit makes sure our groanings in the spirit (not our grumbling, murmuring, or complaining) are ushered into the Throne Room of Heaven. With or without the gift of "Tongues" our prayers in our native language are most welcome in heaven. GOD first loved us; our response of faith, hope, and especially Love is the path to intimacy with Him.

MATTHEW 6:31-33. [The MESSAGE]. "What I'm trying to do here is to get you to relax, to not be so preoccupied with *getting*, so that you can respond to God's *giving*. People who don't know God and the way he works fuss over these things, but you know both God and how he works. Steep your life in God-reality, God-initiative, God-provisions. Don't worry about missing out. You'll find all your everyday human concerns will be met."

Humorous: The only place SUCCESS comes
before WORK is in the dictionary.

"Your ministry is greatly appreciated Man of God.
Keep going on." (Nomsa)

ISAIAH 41:10 – KJV. "Fear thou not; for I am with thee: be not dismayed; for I am thy God: I will strengthen thee; yea, I will help thee; yea, I will uphold thee with the right hand of my righteousness."

JEREMIAH 29:12-13. [The MESSAGE]. "When you call on me, when you come and pray to me, I'll listen. When you come looking for me, you'll find me. Yes, when you get serious about finding me and want it more than anything else, I'll make sure you won't be disappointed."

Faith:
GALATIANS 2:20 – The MESSAGE. "I am
no longer driven to impress God."

My 'Medical Patient Advocate, Michi,' challenged me: "Why are you concerned with perfectionism at all? You have the picture of Jesus, the Prince of Peace, from the artist 'Akiane.' Aim to become Christ-like. Only Jesus is perfect. Spend time in conversation with Him."

What in my opinion can make a church grow in number – membership?

The shepherd relies on the Person of the Chief Shepherd (and is not a hireling). This Pastor preaches the Truths of the Bible without trying to tickle ears. The sheep are taught to be disciples also. LOVE (God's Love for us) is primary. There should be less emphasis on programs and more time spent on ministering to people's needs. All is couched in Prayer!!! God is less concerned with numbers than the reality that the sheep are fed and protected. Signs, miracles, deliverances: these promote Godliness. The demonstration of God's Power will draw in the doubters. There is Dynamic Power in Preaching the Bible message.

From 'Edson C' in South Africa: "I get it,
touching heaven – changing lives."

Harvest Fruit:

1ST CORINTHIANS 2:4-5. [KJV]. "And my speech and my preaching was not with enticing words of man's wisdom, but in demonstration of the Spirit and of power. (5) That your faith should not stand in the wisdom of men, but in the power of God."

Prayer to God is Intercessory Prayer. Prayer with God is time well spent in developing Intimacy. The challenge remains: "How much time are you or I willing to spend directly in communication with THE THREE IN ONE each day?" Remember the value of music.

What does inspiration do?!

It started 'Solomon' on a course of WISDOM. When God asked him what he would like from Him, Solomon asked for 'Wisdom' to guide and lead the Chosen People of God, the undivided Israel and Judah. His father David made him King at age 12.

1ST KINGS 3:9 – KJV. "Give therefore thy servant an understanding heart to judge thy people, that I may discern between good and bad: for who is able to judge this thy so great a people?"

2ND CHRONICLES 1:10 – KJV. "Give me now wisdom and knowledge, that I may go out and come in before this people: for who can judge this thy people, that is so great?"

Q. "How effectively do I use my time?"

Q. "Do I have a plan to go with?"

An incentive Q, building towards greater usefulness for God: "Do I have a vision of what serving God and building the Kingdom is all about?"

According to Dr. Mike Murdock, The WISDOM CENTER (Fort Worth, Texas): It is the questions you ask, not the answers you receive, that has the greater significance.

Invest for the future: Q – "'Dawn,' what are our blue chip stocks in our heavenly bank accounts?"

Q. By investing I mean "where do I spend my capital?" Whenever we sow, we each choose 'fertile ground.' That way our Treasure is ... Kingdom money and Kingdom time. It is also Kingdom love.

MATTHEW 6:21 – KJV. "For where your treasure is, there will your heart be also."

MATTHEW 12:35 – KJV. "A good man out the good treasure of the heart bringeth forth good tidings: and an evil man out of the evil treasure bringeth forth evil things."

LUKE 12:21 – KJV. "So is he that layeth up treasure for himself, and is not rich toward God."

Focus on negative circumstances and you will walk in a life of fear, expecting the worse. Instead, center on THE POSITIVE that our Heavenly Father always provides and the nine fruits of the Holy Spirit will increase within you.

What kind of words does a leader for God speak? Words of praise, words of appreciation, words of encouragement, words of understanding. In summation: words that SPEAK LIFE.

Our words contain Life.

EPHESIANS 4:29 – KJV. "Let no corrupt communication proceed out of your mouth, but that which is good to the use of edifying, that it may minister grace unto the hearers."

EPHESIANS 4:29 – The MESSAGE. "Watch the way you talk. Let nothing foul or dirty come out of your mouth. Say only what helps, each word a gift."

> How does a Shepherd protect his (baa-ad)
> sheep and increase his flock?

By not running scared when the thief, the devil, comes a callin'. By mutual love and respect (for sheep and for Shepherd). By reinforcing the dignity of each person. By not drudging up past wounds. By not judging – instead, by giving constructive advice. By encouraging exercise. By working together to increase "Calmness."

MOMENT-u-M (my 1st autobiography in 2010-2011)

"Keep praising your way through because what you're believing God for is on the way! Even though it didn't happen for you first ... ... you're surely going to be next!!>>>." (Co-Pastor Sheron Strong, Apostolic Truth World Ministries)

> "Madeleine": a name for a snowflake

When snow falls softly
    Crystal flake
God fashions each child

> xx = a girl. xy = a boy

A. Humorous: "Who is the greatest female financier in the Bible?"

B. "Pharoah's daughter. She went to 'the Bank of the Nile' and drew out a little prophet."

1ST CORINTHIANS 13:1 – KJV. "Though I speak with the tongues of men and of angels, and have not charity, I have become as sounding brass, or a tinkling cymbal."

The leader for God realizes it is God's Power that is at work.

1ST CORINTHIANS 2:5 – The MESSAGE. "God's Spirit and God's power did it, which made it clear that your life of faith is a response to God's power, not to some fancy mental or emotional footwork by me or anyone else."

My father who died 6 September 1986 was the role model for my 1st 39 years. Then 'Fr. Frego' took his place as the father figure in my life until he died at the end of January 2010. Both of these men were Dynamic Daily Mass examples. My Dad attended weekday Mass when it was at 7 am and 8 am. Then in his later years it was at 8 am or the exception 7 pm on Thursdays. During the six months I was his 'Legal Assistant in training' he allowed me to start my 8 am workday with 45 minutes of prayer using Rev. Stuart and Jill Briscoe's 150 Psalms with colorful pictures, the Scripture text, and commentary. 'Rev. Stuart' was the Senior Pastor at Elmbrook Church, Brookfield, Wisconsin. This was the home church for my Cousin and her family in Waukesha.

With 'Fr. Frego' I helped chaperone the overnight canoe trip on the Pere Marquette River near Baldwin. We had a dozen teenage boys from Leaton, his mission church while in Rosebush.

After his retirement he shared his apartments in Grand Haven for three day visits; he did all the driving. Incidentally, he drove a motorcycle for recreational purposes for a few years. He also named two dogs "Jo – Jo" after the name 'Josephine.'

In 1989 he and 'Sister Magdalese, S.S.N.D.' (School Sisters of Notre Dame), my Mother and I shared an 11-day vacation, attending the Priestly ordination of his friend in Cheshire, Connecticut. Memorable sightseeing included: Niagara Falls, the MLB Hall of Fame in Cooperstown, Norman Rockwell's magazine covers in Vermont, the NBA Hall of Fame in Hartford, and the NFL Hall of Fame in Canton.

FAITH

> Man's strength is futile
> God's Love is a certainty
> Each day forever

Do not rely on your own power to get 'u' or "U" into the Light.

Accept that you are a sinner and receive JESUS as 'your Savior and Lord.'

> As leaders for God we walk in Light. Light
> has pushed back the Darkness.

LUKE 10:18 – KJV. "And he said to them, I beheld Satan as lightning fall from heaven."

ISAIAH 6:8 – KJV. "Also I heard the voice of the Lord, saying, Whom shall I send, and who will go for us? Then said I, Here am I; send me."

ISAIAH 9:2 – KJV. "The people that walked in darkness have seen a great light: they that dwell in the land of the shadow of death, upon them hath the light shined."

PSALMS 19:8 – The MESSAGE. "The life-maps of God are right, showing the way to joy. The directions of God are plain and easy on the eyes."

PSALMS 119:105 – KJV. "Thy word is a lamp unto my feet, and a light unto my path." This verse inspired 'Amy Grant' to write the music and sing "Thy Word."

PSALMS 119:30 – The MESSAGE. "Break open your words let the light shine out, let ordinary people see the meaning."

1ST JOHN 1:5 – KJV. "This then is the message which we have heard of him, and declare unto you, that God is light, and in him is no darkness at all."

"God has given you a particular kind of personality. He has also created a particular circle of individuals who can be reached and touched by that personality as by none other in the world. And then He shapes and orders your life so as to bring you into contact with that circle."

(STREAMS IN THE DESERT, Vol. 2, August
20, Mrs. Charles E. Cowman)

'Jack Nehmer,' Reed City missionary to Nicaragua, has 1ST JOHN 4:19 as his Facebook Timeline cover top. In the [KJV]: "We love him, because he first loved us."

The weather in Big Rapids ideally is: "sunny and 80 degrees."

A leader for God flows in the things of God. Children, teenagers, young adults, senior citizens have to have "Incentives." They also need love and affection.

> As we sow to Destiny we reap for Destiny
> (MATTHEW 6:33; 7:7-11)
> Music => => => !! ~~~ !!

'Pastor Joe' encouraged me to write: "Let's get souls into the Kingdom by the writing." I was a literary evangelist long before I became "the Knight of the Word."

> A faith declaration: "Where He leads me, I will
> follow. I'll go with Him all the way."
> "God is preparing for where he is taking you
> to!!!!!" (Co-Pastor Sheron Strong)

If God brought you to it, He'll bring you through it. If the devil brought you to it (a Temptation), then God will provide a way of escape.

From: 'Walt & Sophie Novak,' Catholic Charismatic leaders in Big Rapids

(Ron), "God needs you right where you are."

1ST PETER 4:11b, c. [KJV]. "; if any man minister, let him do it as of the ability which God giveth: that God in all things may be glorified through Jesus Christ, to whom be praise and dominion for ever and ever. Amen."

Humorous facts of Nature: Butterflies taste with their feet. Hummingbirds can't walk. Kangaroos can't walk backwards.

Sightseeing adds to one's education. Fresno, California, is home to Yosemite Nat'l Park. I've only visited the Great Salt Lake in Utah, Pike's Peak in Colorado, Yellowstone Nat'l Park in Wyoming, and Glacier Nat'l Park in Montana.

What advice did my 1st Cousin Mark, a Yooper, give me?
"When in difficult times look back on past
successes and be thankful to God."

The joy of the Lord – 1, 6-26-2014

We will kick this off with NEHEMIAH, chapter 1.

> NEHEMIAH 8:10c – KJV. "; for the joy
> of the LORD is your strength."

Commentary on NEHEMIAH 1: If a person lives 20 years without a dour, sorrowful face and that is how a marriage goes for 20 years that is a POWERFUL testimony for God. My Parents (Albin & Kathleen) lived 41 years, 10 ½ months this way.

> 'Darren' defines joy: "The abundance of
> His Presence with perfect Peace."

ECCLESIASTES 2:26 – KJV. "For God giveth to a man that is good in his sight wisdom, and knowledge, and joy: but to the sinner he giveth travail, to gather and to heap up, that he may give to him that is good before God. This also is vanity and vexation of spirit."

The reign of Jehoshaphat

2ND CHRONICLES 20:20b-21. [KJV]. "Believe in the LORD your God, so shall ye be established; believe his prophets, so shall ye prosper. (21) And when he had consulted with the people, he appointed singers unto the LORD, and that should praise the beauty of holiness, as they went out before the army, and to say, Praise the LORD; for his mercy endureth for ever."

Keep Pastor's soul in order. I want to live in my assignment.

PSALMS 30:5 – KJV. "For his anger endureth but for a moment; in his favour is life: weeping may endure for a night, but joy cometh in the morning."

SALVATION: "Converted unto Jesus."

REDEMPTION: "Release secured by payment – the blood of Jesus Christ."

What goes into the covenant of Marriage?

Days, weeks, months, even years of building friendship !! ~ ~ ~ !! .

Honoring THE THREE IN ONE in thought, speech, music, and actions <> .

Mutual trust (remembering that both participants have a past history with baggage)

Unconditional love; the dream of many years of Joy and Peace together; knowing that God's paradise is at the end of the rainbow.

  Q. "How does a person share?"
  R. **** With appropriateness ****

[Be careful.]
"What do you want me to be careful about?"
[LIFE]
God's approval is the center of LIFE.

Everything we do, the way we see, the entire world the entire universe, Everything on earth has

LIFE because of God. He is the Beginning and the End, the Alpha and Omega, true glorious GOD. He is always faithful, always loving, always waiting on our needs and cares.

He does not expect us to repay Him, just know love and serve Him. Have that intimate relationship with Him. Do all to the glory of God.

How might I seize LIFE?

Seize means to capture, gain control, to take the bull by the horns. In another sense it means: be enthusiastic, work hard, use diplomacy to calm others down. Certainly, it is not me alone trying for Victory. Jesus wants me to invite Him on this quest. He is far better equipped and prepared for this kind of soldiery.

The ordination of 'Rev. Joseph N. Cottle'

On Sunday 15 July 2007 'Pastor Joe' was ordained in Midland, Michigan by 'Dr. Mark T. Barclay' in a 5 pm ceremony. 'Rev. Joe to be' preached a 50 minute message at Revival Christian Center (RCC) aka Christ's Harvest Ministries earlier that day in their Morning Service.

IF you have time to pray, God has time to listen.

PSALMS 40:2 – KJV. "He brought me up also out of an horrible pit, out of the miry clay, and set my feet upon a rock, and established my goings."

ROMANS 14:17 – KJV. "For the kingdom of God is not meat and drink; but righteousness, and peace, and joy in the Holy Ghost."

2ND CORINTHIANS 4:7 – KJV. "But we have this treasure in earthen vessels, that the excellency of the power may be of God, and not of us."

The blessing of the Good Lord be upon you!

HABAKKUK 2:4b – KJV. ": but the just shall live by his faith."

HABAKKUK 2:4b – The MESSAGE. "But the person in right standing before God through loyal and steady believing is fully alive, really alive."

"Enjoy the whether": whether or not I
get married within five years
To rejoice is to reactivate Joy.
A move of God takes place because people,
many people, are praying.
"Don't quit! … Don't stop! … God is
turning it around in your favor!!!!!"
To 'Dawn': "You're beautiful! Very beautiful!!"
[I appreciate that.]

HEBREWS 10:35-36. [KJV]. "Cast not away therefore your confidence, which hath great recompence of reward. (36) For ye have need of patience, that, after ye have done the will of God, ye might receive the promise."

Live well; Live wisely.

JAMES 3:17 – KJV. "But the wisdom that is from above is first pure, then peaceable, gentle, and easy to be intreated, full of mercy and good fruits, without partiality, and without hypocrisy."

ISAIAH 40:31 – The MESSAGE. "But those who wait upon GOD get fresh strength. They spread their wings and soar like eagles, They run and don't get tired, they walk and don't lag behind."

1ST JOHN 2:17b. [KJV]. ": but he (she) that doeth the will of God abideth for ever."

My Pastor, 'Rev. Joe,' represents THE THREE IN ONE and guides me along the Highway of Holiness. He is a Word-man Pastor. I am thankful that he directs souls preparing them to get past former troubles and focus on right living and it begins "Now."

Q. "What is worse than going to Hell permanently?"

A. "Nothing."

Q. Would it be worse if you took someone with you?

A. Suppose that person is your spouse.

A. "In Hell you suffer alone. There is no such thing as husbands and wives suffering together." Each person there is in individual agony and will go into 'the Lake of Fire' after the Final Judgment.

The Lake of Fire will smell like rotten eggs, that is, the only smell you can't get rid of or use to: "burning sulpher."

What testimony can 'Dawn and I' share?

REVELATION 3:8 – KJV. "I know thy works: behold, I have set before thee an open door, and no one can shut it: for thou hast a little strength, and hast kept my word, and hast not denied my name."

For Potential Marriages: Pastor Joe's question
"Are you patient enough to do it God's way?"
The 2nd century theologian 'Irenaeus' said: "The glory
of God is a human being who is fully alive."
"Love begins at home." ☺ + ☺.
"There has never been a sunset that
was not followed by a dawn."

'Dawn' is a fan of soccer. She played it in high school. She likes it because it always is physically demanding. She is not a fan of basketball.

Why do I enjoy MLB so much?

"Pitch after pitch, strike after strike, every inning is a mixture of strength, concentration and strategy." (Internet finding concerning 'baseball.')

"When we believe in God's plan for us,
every age is the perfect age to be."
(Birthday card 2-22-2000 from my
brother Gary and his wife Sue)

Integrity keeps promises. Observe God!

NUMBERS 23:19 – KJV. "God is not a man, that he should lie; neither the son of Man, that he should repent: hath he said, and shall he not do it? or hath he spoken, and shall he not make it good?"

This Scripture is the 1ˢᵗ memory verse on Wednesday night taught by Pastor Dale Murray's wife Roberta at Pine Chapel in 1993 just after I joined their congregation in Blanchard (Montcalm County). 'Roberta and I' share the same 2/22 birthday. We have celebrated together since 1994.

HEALING (from schizophrenia disorder, bipolar type)
"You will be healed."
(Or I will function so well that the enemy,
Satan, ... is totally defeated)

Hear, feel, and know you are not alone.

ISAIAH 55:12 – KJV. "For ye shall go out with joy and be led forth with peace: the mountains and hills shall break forth before you into singing; and all the trees of the field shall clap their hands."

PSALMS 35:27 – KJV. "Let them shout for joy, and be glad, that favour my righteous cause: yea, let them say continually, Let the LORD be magnified, which hath pleasure in the prosperity of his servant."

SHARING A TESTIMONY:

"...We are told to preach the Gospel – not our own experience. It's God Word that will do the trick, but it helps to put 'windows' into our teaching to let people 'see into' the Truth and that's what a testimony can do." (Thank You For Being a Friend, Jill Briscoe, page 96)

In your next year(s) may you enjoy more and more the abundant life, the zoe life, that only JESUS brings that will fill and satisfy you.

5 a.m. Morning Prayer: to become more Christ-like

PSALMS 17:15 – KJV. "As for me, I will behold thy face in righteousness: I shall be satisfied, when I awake, with thy likeness."

What is "Courage"? It is "mental or moral strength to venture, persevere, and withstand danger, fear, or difficulty." *(Webster's Seventh New Collegiate Dictionary)*

FAITH: "Fantastic Adventures In Trusting Him"

Q. How are we created in the image and likeness of God?

A. As one of my relatives pointed out: "We do all the things God does, but in lesser manner and to a lesser degree."

Let me elaborate. We create (our work). We talk (with or to God) (and also to human beings and to animals). We eat (Jesus enjoyed bread and fish). We rest (God rested on the 7th day. Jesus fell asleep in the boat after telling His apostles, "Let's go to the other side": He wasn't going to go to the middle of the lake and then sink.) We have eternity (either with God in heaven or with the fallen angels in the Lake of Fire). We have the ability to listen!!! We also have the ability to Love.

What is Dawn's advice in order to live each new day separate from the carry over that yesterday's memory ingrained? [Don't think about it.]

If God is in control, I don't have to be. What does this mean? The devil tries to be in control, and ever since Adam's sin evil in the world has occurred. God, however, is directing history (moment by moment, breath by breath); all is for God's glory. He is preparing for Jesus' triumphal return and the marriage feast of the Lamb.

Good Fruit

PSALMS 118:8 – KJV. "It is better to trust in the LORD than to put confidence in man."

PSALMS 118:8 – The MESSAGE. "Far better to take refuge in GOD than trust in people;."

(PSALMS 118 is Dawn's favorite Psalm.)
Since May 2013 I have prayed a minimum
of 20 minutes each day for 'Dawn.'
Verbal Language (without commenting on 'body language'):

JUDE 20 – KJV. "But ye, beloved, building up yourselves on your most holy faith, praying in the Holy Ghost,.."

JUDE 20-21. [The MESSAGE]. "But you, dear friends, carefully build yourselves up in this most holy faith by praying in the Holy

Spirit, staying right at the center of God's love, keeping your arms open and outstretched, ready for the mercy of our Master, Jesus Christ. This is the unending life, the real life!"

We dream Big, Bigger, Best!!!! God surpasses all of this when reality becomes future.

'Gary Chapman' in his THE FIVE LOVE LANGUAGES identifies these five love languages: (1) Words of Affirmation; (2) Quality Time; (3) Receiving Gifts; (4) Acts of Service; (5) Physical Touch.

'Judson J. Swihart' in his How Do You Say, "I Love You"? describes eight languages of expressing love in marriage:

(1) meeting material needs; (2) helping; (3) spending time together; (4) meeting emotional needs; (5) saying it with words; (6) saying it with touch; (7) being on the same side; (8) bringing out the best.

His thesis is that we must recognize our own languages and that of our spouse and make sure that we aren't speaking "foreign languages" whose meanings aren't understood. I agree.

PSALMS 126:2 – KJV. "Then was our mouth filled with laughter, and our tongue with singing: then said they among the heathen, The LORD hath done great things for them."

"If you abide in Me, ..."

JOHN 15:11 – KJV. "These things have I spoken unto you, that my joy might remain in you, and that your joy might be full."

JOHN 15:11 – The MESSAGE. "I've told you these things for a purpose: that my joy might be your joy, and your joy wholly mature."

Q. What could we learn from 'Mary L. Clark'?

A. I learned that Busyness, the lessening of Quality Time, no longer mentioning the positives, allowing your mind to be bombarded by the unimportant IS satan's plan to steal your peace, kill your walk, and destroy your (covenant) marriage. God is the silver lining when all looks bleak."

Humorous. To the captain of the battleship that got stuck on a reef just off the Philippines in 2013 and just got pulled to safety: from his commanding officer, "Where did you get your driver's license? out of a cracker-jack-box?"

The dignity and sanctity of Marriage

PROVERBS 5:15 – KJV. "Drink waters out of thine own cistern, and running waters out of thine own well."

THE GOOD WIFE:

PROVERBS 31:12 – KJV. "She will do him good and not evil all the days of her life."

Q. Do you realize you have 11 Yoplait yogurts?

A. Yes!! Ten for me and one for 'Dawn' to take to work. Her favorite is 'Harvest Peach.'

"You're a good man." (Commendable, virtuous, just)

Some 'girls' are blessed and highly favored by God: "Patrizia, Angel A, Dawn" is one of them.

God, how can I have the greatest impact for You?

I believe in "Divine Appointments" even when they be be 'literary.' For some people reading and praying with their favorite devotional is a "God appointment." My goal is to teach and change lives for the Kingdom of God.

What about compliments?

Words of appreciation (verbal compliments) are encouraging words, kind words, humble words. They build up the other person; they do not tear down. It goes far deeper than saying, "I love you." Eye contact is also a very important compliment.

Michigan has four distinct seasons: spring, summer, autumn, winter. We progress from a time of new beginnings, to a time of growth, to reaping the harvest of hard work, to a time of rest.

"Faith means taking one step at a time totally trusting the promise that God will do for me what I could never do for myself."

Begin or continue to sow 'Kindness' that you would like given to you.

Be ready whether it is "in season" or 'out of season.'

What have I learned about the dignity and sanctity of life?

LIFE BEGINS AT CONCEPTION. The female (xx) contributes 'the egg' on her regular menstrual cycle. The male (xy) contributes 'the sperm.' As God decides, a child may or may not be produced. An ultrasound is able to detect the heart-beat at 18 days.

Every embryo, fetus, child, teenager, young adult, parent, teacher, senior citizen continues to be alive and growing until his or her last breath is taken.

Sharing takes place inside the womb as the pre-born begins to kick his or her mother's belly. Remember, 'the umbilical cord' is a cord arising from the navel that connects the fetus with the placenta.

As a baby that child will feed off milk. Then there is language development. Communication inside and outside the womb is both verbal and non-verbal. As a baby, "crying" is a great motivator to get "needs-met."

As we grow we learn more things such as facts and promises. We begin to build relationships. We learn trust and sharing love. Our knowledge and experience of God escalates.

My faith is no longer my parents' faith. It is the faith as an adult that I have freely chosen. I believe my healing from "schizophrenia disorder, bipolar type" is a living Testimony of God working within me. "I am on Fire for God!" The Holy Spirit lives within me as I am 'a Temple of the Holy Spirit.'

Also very important: "Know who your allies are!" On the night of Jesus' crucifixion the Gospel of John narrates that it was 'Joseph of Aramathaea' and 'Nicodemus' who were the allies for Jesus. These two Jews took Jesus down from the cross, used about 100 pounds of myrrh and aloes, and laid him in a new sepulcher.

ROMANS 12:21 – KJV. "Be not overcome of evil, but overcome evil with good."

"God is bringing you into a new & fruitful place! … The place where you are going is not like the place you've been … It's so much better!!!!!" (Co-Pastor Sheron Strong)

Mature righteousness consists of faith, love, peace.

PSALMS 18:30 – The MESSAGE. "What a God! His road stretches straight and smooth. Every God-direction is road tested. Everyone who runs toward him Makes it."

"Together" is a powerful word in the Spirit realm. It means you, me, and God. With this combination, this three-some, everything is possible as it is centered in Unity with God.

"Holiness"" has a price tag and it does not get marked down for 'Black Friday,' the day after U.S.A. Thanksgiving Day, the 4th Thursday of November.

In my vocabulary 'MOMENT-u-M' for a pre-born is the Selection of Godly Names. "Keith, Keith" is pronounced by 'the blowing of air from my mouth.' On a Baby Name card at 'Living Water Christian Resource Center, Inc.' in downtown Big Rapids "Keith" means "Brave." This is the closest I can come to "Courage" in a repeated name.

I put Christ 1st in my life.
I went where the Bible and the Holy Spirit told me, "GO."

Pray about everything. Pray about everything.
Pray about everyone!

Listen for the confirming inner voice of the Holy Spirit. If it is not there, then do not move ahead and act. The appropriate timing will manifest itself.

1ST CHRONICLES 17:2 – KJV. "Then Nathan said unto David, Do all that is in thine heart; for God is with thee."

On Wednesday 2 January 2013 retired 'Chief Master Sergeant Mark S. Brejcha' treated me to breakfast at "Wild Rose Café" next to Currie's BP gas station. While in the process of doing errands he stopped to show me the World War I memorial at FERRIS. He then pointed out that two 'Ferris Institute' students with names "in memorial of" are the basis for our airport name, "Roben-Hood Airport."

Do I need a blood transfusion where God-worth replaces my self-worth? I asked God to fill me with 'a sense of His wholeness.' I know SIN is "missing His mark." My perfectionism is being replaced by greater self-tolerance even as I hold on to my trait of "being a stickler for details."

What is needed to be a God-type writer?

"Word, structure, form." Word is the Bible. In JOHN 1:1-3 Jesus is the Word. Structure is the approach, the format we use. Form as a verb means "create."

"Accountability, discipline, report" is another trio. Report means 'eye-witness accounts.'

'Dr. Mike Murdock,' author of SEEDS of WISDOM TOPICAL BIBLE, teaches that we are planting seeds for a harvest (and naming our seeds) when we tithe or give Offerings: whether it be – time, love, patience, wisdom, and / or money. Everybody needs to maintain BALANCE in their lives. Not everything needs to be done at once. Do get proper Rest and Nutrition.

Leisure

In American English a "plum" is something excellent or superior. The color of the fruit (the plum) is dark reddish purple. My only 'plum' is "Patrizia" – a term of endearment.

In the detective board game "CLUE" the winner is the 1st person who correctly identifies the murderer, the murder weapon, and the room where the murder took place. "Professor Plum" is never 'the antagonist' (the murderer).

[Sweet dreams] – Dawn's "Good night" blessing

On Monday 30 September 2013 I woke up at 5:01 a.m. (atomic clock) thinking about Summer Olympics. 'Running' was my event to win a medal. There were two tiers of competitors (1st thru 8th and 9th thru 16th). In my dream I was in the top "8" twice and 'the running rabbit' in another race in order to maximize their efforts. When I woke up I knew that I had competed WELL and furthered good sportsmanship. I certainly helped others to feel good about themselves. That pleased God and I was joyful.

Who is this JESUS, the Child of Light?

JOHN 20:30-31. [KJV]. "And many other signs truly did Jesus in the presence of his disciples, which are not written in this book: (31) But these are written, that ye might believe that Jesus is the Christ, the Son of God; and that believing ye might have life through his name."

Highlights of joy in the early Church, as recorded in ACTS

ACTS 8:8 – KJV. "And there was great joy in that city (Philip in Samaria)."

ACTS 13:52 – KJV. "And the disciples were filled with joy, and with the Holy Ghost." (Arriving in Iconium)

ACTS 20:24 – KJV. "But none of these things move me, neither count I my life dear unto myself, so that I might finish my course with joy, and the ministry, which I have received of the Lord Jesus, to testify the gospel of the grace of God."

[You get a good night's sleep]: From 'Dawn'

PSALMS 5:3 – KJV. "My voice shalt thou hear in the morning, O LORD; in the morning will I direct my prayer unto thee, and will look up."

The Christian journey / adventure is not a sprint, but a marathon of 26.2 miles (26 miles, 385 yards) of living and loving. It is important that we enjoy this journey and handle 'the whethers' as life changing decisions that God has in His novel for each of us.

It is a proven fact: "HUGS reduce Stress."

Productivity – 1, 7-02-2014

The Spirit of the Living God is at work.

Did you dedicate July 2014 to God? My Uncle 'Jake the Peddler' was born on July 2, 1924 and lived 74 years, dying of 'lung cancer,' and he had a personal relationship with Jesus. In 1987, a year after my Dad died, he thanked 'Albin' for his long hours in Prayer for him. He told me, "Your Dad prayed long and hard for me. I'll be eternally grateful."

PSALMS 145:18 – KJV. "The LORD is nigh unto all them that call upon him, to all that call upon him in truth."

PSALMS 145:18 – The MESSAGE. "God's there, listening for all who pray, for all who pray and mean it."

From 'Dawn': [Write on]

PROVERBS 21:5 – The MESSAGE. "Careful planning puts you ahead in the long run; hurry and scurry puts you further behind."

GOD examines our motives.
You cannot grow without going on with God.

From 'Pastor Joe': Friends bring comfort and act as cheerleaders. Even the coach helps me get through the now. However, both the coach and the mentor's job are to get me to the next level. They push me to activate my greater Potential. They see my future.

The world advertises: "I'm your Boss. Let's talk Productivity."

"I declare Productivity in Jesus Mighty name!"

An incentive question: "Do you, do I have a vision as we build towards greater usefulness for God?"

Get Serious!

PROVERBS 16:10-11. [The MESSAGE]. "A good leader motivates, doesn't mislead, doesn't exploit. God cares about honesty in the workplace; your business is his business."

I asked 'Dawn' what quality she is looking for in her Boss.
She replied: [Understanding]

MARK 1:15 – KJV. "And saying, The time is fulfilled, and the kingdom of God is at hand: repent ye, and believe the gospel."

Birthday greetings to my Medical Patient Advocate, 'Michi,' of "Shiloh Pines." Do receive ALL the Blessings GOD has prepared for you. Let Him enlarge your territory. I know JESUS is your Best Friend. Thank you for the 'Akiane' "Prince of Peace" picture.

Q. "Do you have a working definition of Hope?"

A. "Hope is knowing all is going to end well in Christ (and Jesus will be there no matter what comes to take you through it)."

PROVERBS 9:9-10. [KJV]. "Give instruction to a wise man, and he will be yet wiser: teach a just man, and he will increase in learning. (10) The fear of the LORD is the beginning of wisdom: and the knowledge of the holy is understanding."

PROVERBS 9:9-10. [The MESSAGE]. "Save your breath for the wise – they'll be wiser for it; tell good people what you know – they'll profit from it. Skilled living gets its start in the Fear-of-GOD, insight into life from knowing a Holy God."

How did I get my start in the Marketplace?

At age 12 I agreed to sell 'the Pioneer' (Big Rapids newspaper) on Mondays through Fridays for "7 cents." I picked up my newspapers at the back of 'the Pioneer' (where the Emporium is now). Each day at 4 p.m. I stood at the entrance / exit of Hanchett's Manufacturing. No one gave me a larger tip than $ .25 for a newspaper. I banked my money at 1st National Bank (now Chemical Bank) and used my savings for a two week Boy Scout National Jamboree in 1960 at Colorado Springs, Colorado.

By the time I decided I wanted my own six day paper route my Brother Gary already had 'the Marion Avenue route.' This left me all the territory from Bridge Street to Rose to Sheridan, the job I held until joining the seminary in Grand Rapids in September 1961.

1ST CORINTHIANS 2:9 – KJV. "But as it is written, Eye hath not seen, nor ear heard, neither hath entered the heart of man, the things which God hath prepared for those who love him."

Monday afternoons at "SJV" (September 1967-May 1969)
Developing communication skills as a teacher

In the Buffalo area Monday afternoons meant a bus ride for
our seminarians to our designated schools to teach catechism
to students on the shared time release program. Students were
bused to Catholic Schools for "Religious Ed" for the final hour
on Mondays. For my first six weeks I was a team-teacher with
'Father' Frank C (a Hospital Chaplain 'Doing Well' in 1989). We
taught 30 7th grade boys at O.L.V. After six weeks I became a
roving substitute teacher in all grades (7th-12th) all-boys, all-girls,
mixed. Each week had its own challenges.

In September 1968-May 1969 I taught 28 – 7th grade boys at
Our Lady of Victory (O.L.V.) in Lackawanna, N.Y. The rule for
teaching all-boys was to compile a list of my students' birthdays
on the 1st day of class and then send them a card on their birthday.
I did this. I expected intangible results (although seven or eight
sent me a Christmas card to East Aurora, N.Y.) Scripture says in
PROVERBS 22:6 – KJV. "Train up a child in the way he should
go: and when he is old, he will not depart from it." I let God work
on their hearts at some future time, remembering this surprise
gift, drawing them closer to 'Abba' because of it. (If you had an
all-girls class receiving birthday cards they would think you were
in love with them.)

Years later in Bay City, Michigan, my friend who sold insurance,
'Fred Johnson,' sent me yearly birthday cards (1978-1984). He
also gave me a set of 'jumper cables' for my car.

My Grandmother, 'Eunice Grebin Trainor,' praised my thought-
fulness in sending just the right birthday cards to enhance her

Special Day. She passed on to be with the Lord, I think it was 1983, at the age of '92.'

The Boy Scouts help train young people to be Successful Adults. The 12 Scout Laws: Trustworthy, loyal, helpful, courteous, kind, obedient, cheerful, thrifty, brave, clean, and reverent (I am missing one) and their slogan: "Do a good turn daily": these are core values that strengthen God's Ten Commandments and increase 'Integrity.'

Life changing experiences

My Mother and Dad needed a vacation during the summer of 1962. We left Iron Mountain with the promise that Dad would phone Grandpa "collect" every night to check on Grandma in the Veteran's Hospital in Kingsford, MI. We traveled the northern route with our Tent / Trailer. We visited Mount Rushmore in South Dakota, the Calgary Stampede, Glacier Nat'l Park, Banff and Jasper Nat'l Parks, and Lake Louise. On our final Monday in Canada a black bear visited us for our picnic lunch. When Dad phoned Grandpa that same afternoon, he accepted the call for the first time. 'Grandma Clara' had passed away on Sunday. We hurried to Calgary and Dad caught a flight to Milwaukee, and then a flight to Iron Mountain. We camped at the Calgary Airport but left our two metal poles in their parking lot. We bought two wooden poles the next night as Mom drove Gary and I to her Parents in Waconia, Minnesota.

I was a seminary high school junior in English class with Fr. Ancona (later Monsignor Ancona) the Friday afternoon 'President John F. Kennedy' was assassinated, 22 November 1963 in Dallas, Texas. Classes were cancelled on Monday so we could watch the funeral on TV. 'President JFK' is a hero of mine as is bipolar 'President Abraham Lincoln."

George Washington was born on February 11, 1732 at Bridges' Creek, "Wakefield Plantation," Westmoreland County, Virginia. When the calendar was revised in 1752, eleven days were added so the birth date became "2-22-1732," New Style. When my maternal Grandmother 'Eunice' learned that her daughter had a son born on February 22nd she surmised: "Now we have a George." Her two great grandfathers were named 'George.'

PUT ON CHRIST

What is the Gospel message to share?

Go tell it on the mountain and over the hills and everywhere that Jesus Christ is born and lives today. JESUS loves you. Now tell this message of the Lord to your neighbors. (Bishop Caleb Don Crigger and his wife Brenda – Theodore, Alabama, six miles south of downtown Mobile)

"Stop stressing about stuff that really doesn't matter at all. Just seek ye 1st the Kingdom of God and everything else will fall into place." (Pastor Spence, near Atlanta – Georgia)

I was partially healed from the generational curse based on the time and the number "10:01" that Wednesday night before I joined the New Journey Clubhouse Team traveling to Kalamazoo in September 2000. 'Tia' prayed a Prayer of Benediction over me and the other seven 'non-whites' also laid hands on me. Even though I take medicine in 2014 I realize I am at the point God wants me to be for now.

Q. 'Father Lam Le' asked me after a luncheon at Applebee's: "Do I hold any grudges against the Catholic Church or my Parents?"

A. "Not any more."

"Y.": We are a functional family devoted to the Blessed or Holy Trinity. I have always loved my Dad and Mom. They both did what they thought was right to raise me to be a Catholic priest. In the Bigger picture I can do more sharing the Gospel as a literary evangelist.

> "If a Church wants a better Pastor, it can get
> one by praying for the one that it has."

Fantasy weekend with my Dad: You tell me when?

We went to old Tiger Stadium just the two of us for the weekend. We saw the Saturday afternoon and Sunday matinee games. I don't need to recall Detroit's opponent. We spent Saturday night in a Detroit Hotel. Saturday after supper we went for a walk. I don't remember any of the conversation, just his presence!!!

When I was age 8 my Dad had taken our family to 'Tiger Stadium at the corner of Michigan and Trumble' for a Sunday afternoon doubleheader versus the New York Yankees. LHP 'Whitey Ford' pitched the 1st game. 'Yogi Berra' (catcher) and 'Mickey Mantle' (centerfield) played both games.

JAMES 1:2 – KJV. "Blessed is the man that endureth temptation: for when he is tried, he shall receive the crown of life, which the Lord hath promised to them that love him."

LUKE 8:15 – KJV. "But that on good ground are they, which in an honest and good heart, having heard the word, keep it, and bring forth fruit with patience."

"God desires that we respond to him with thankfulness, authenticity, honesty, and passion." (The MESSAGE // Remix: Solo – An Uncommon Devotional, page 362)

From 'Darren': "Be well, Be whole, Be full of wisdom, And God bless you."

"Age" is not as important as 'Maturity.' For me this is what I think goes into 'Maturity.' Maturity begins with intelligence and clarity of meaning of spoken words. Does the other person make you feel GOOD about yourself and your personality? Does that other person draw you closer to Mighty God? Furthermore, are both of you willing to Sacrifice to make the relationship grow firmer and bond together for the long-term?

From 'Dawn': [What are you doing?]
The deeper question: "HOW DOES JESUS KNOW ME?"
This is where "Relationship" and "Intimacy"
come into 'Maximum quality.'

How did I get to Bay City?

From August 1976 – May 13, 1977 I worked as the Assistant Manager at 'Town Finance' in Big Rapids. In January 1977 they raised my pay from $3.00 per hour to $3.10 an hour. During that nine month time span I worked for two different Managers.

Probably my most unusual job assignment was to make 'a Collection Chase' to East Tawas (over 100 miles away). After lunch I located his trailer. Then I waited. Finally, I walked up to his front entrance, and the laundry woman from 'Greenridge Nursing Home' (now 'Metron') met me. I worked at 'Greenridge' as a male orderly from 7 a.m. – 3:30 p.m. as my 1st job after my first hospitalization for schizophrenia in late summer 1973. It was a two year growth period for punching a time card and wearing a name tag with my white shirt and white pants.

In August 1977 the Principal at Bay City All Saints high school invited me to interview as a Potential Religion Teacher. For lunch he treated me at 'The Char Haus.' Yes, I was hired without sending any resumes to the Saginaw diocese. This move (90 miles) required Faith that God would take care of the details. I filled my green 'Cutlass Supreme' and left "Ur" like 'Abram and Sarai.' Seven years later my father invited me back to "BR" to become his Legal Assistant in Training.

Evaluate yourself as a teacher at Bay City All Saints

I taught "Morality & Spirit Seekers" at the north campus beginning at 10 a.m. to juniors and one senior who needed an extra Religion credit to graduate. We made this class "FUN" at the very beginning. Instead of all the desks facing west we rotated them to all face north. 'Craig Goslin' sat in the front row. We became "eternal friends" in early October 1977.

After lunch at the south campus (a ten minute walk for students at the north campus) I tried to teach two classes of "Freshmen Religion – core curriculum." Permanent Deacon 'Rick Howard' also taught "Freshmen Religion" all day. My downfall was my inability to handle "Discipline" with freshmen. I lasted until Thanksgiving break in November.

Interestingly, it snowed 20-24 inches the night before our 'Morality semester exam.' The grading system for that Class was "PASS or FAIL." My final question: "Why do you deserve credit for this class?" All my students 'PASSED.' I had only signed a contract to teach 1st semester.

St. Laurent Bros.: my favorite Bay City workplace

I started at the cash register in early October. After Halloween I packed candy and dates for Christmas in 1978 and 1979. Then I roasted peanuts in their wholesale department as a Union Member for 14-15 months. As the last person hired, I was the first to be 'let go.'

The 2nd floor oven was about six feet long with a conveyor belt about 22 feet where the nuts were lightly salted before dropping into a separate cart for each species. I cooked diete and blanched peanuts, cashews, almonds, filberts, Brazil nuts, and pecans. Our 'Foreman' Alex Tobias was the only person allowed to roast the 10 pounds of Macadamia nuts from Hawaii. He did this every two months. In order to get the nuts into the hopper and moving through the cooker I took the elevator to the 3rd floor and used my jackknife to open the string-fastened 100 pound bags. Having a keen eye for the color of the cooking nuts allowed me to adjust the speed of the cooking. Therefore, I 'turned out' consistently very good product.

On my birthday in 1980 "I had to bring the donuts from Essexville for the 10 a.m. break." After work I headed to "BR" for the Elk's Fish Fry and ordered the shrimp dinner. That was the Friday U.S.A. defeated Russia "4-3" in 'the Lake Placid, N.Y., Winter Olympics.' On Sunday we won the impossible gold medal. MARK

11:23 – KJV. "For verily I say unto you, That whomsoever shall say to this mountain, Be thou removed, and be thou cast into the sea; and shall not doubt in his heart, … ; he shall have whatsoever he saith."

What do you do when the U.S. economy is laying off people and you lose your best paying, most FUN job? It became Reality for me in early 1981. As I was collecting "Unemployment Benefits" I joined JOB CLUB. When they tested my reading comprehension, I tested "13.8" – sophomore in College. When I was a II-College seminarian at Aquinas College in Grand Rapids I had the choice of one elective a semester. I chose the Business Majors road: Economics 201, 202. My Professor marked on a curve, and I scored an "A" in my 1st semester. Years later in Big Rapids I learned that 'theology' and 'economics' are polar opposites. What job did I apply for while attending JOB CLUB? I wanted to become "a Stockbroker" at A.G. Edwards in downtown Bay City. Later I applied in Saginaw to become "a Travel Agent." Because of the locations I had personally visited inside and outside the U.S.A. the Lady interviewer said she would put my resume and application at the top of … the application pile (a polite way to say that soon another person would be the top candidate).

The U.S. Coast Guard in Essexville

After my "Unemployment Benefits" were used up I went on 'Public Assistance.' I spent 13 weeks at the Coast Guard doing various jobs, but not as the cook they expected to have who would be able to bake 'cakes.' To save gasoline costs I rode two buses to Essexville (the neighboring town) and then walked a mile from the bus stop to the Coast Guard. That was good morning and afternoon exercise. I did not like or enjoy the 13 weeks at the Coast Guard.

Working for a season at 'Liberty Technology'

When a new opportunity arose to sell cleaning products at 'Liberty Technology' on the west side of the Saginaw River in Bay City I joined them. After a season at 'Liberty Technology' I turned my life over to God again, and He provided the job as 'Church secretary' for Pastor Ross Lakes, an Indiana native, at HOUSE OF PRAISE.

15 months at 'House of Praise'

It was there that I met 'Anita,' a young General Motors secretary living in Saginaw and commuting to Bay City to this Pentecostal church. I was no longer attending Mass. 15 months later everyone said: "It is the opportunity of a lifetime" to return to Big Rapids, live in an upstairs apartment across the alley from my Parents, and work with my father in his LAW offices.

Six months: "How did I help my father as his 'legal assistant in training'"?

First of all, at age 64 he was very alert, conscientious, and God-centered. He needed me to be 'his hands and his feet.' This meant errands to City Hall and the Mecosta County Courthouse. Secondly, he did complex tax returns and counseling for saving future tax dollars. He had me doing adding machine work to pull together tax data for itemizing. Thirdly, as a notary public I was able to go with him to a client's house "after hours" on a Friday to make sure that this gentleman had peace of mind about his 'Last Will and Testament.' This man died within 48 hours. I took 'Inventory' of all his goods so his house and all its contents were ready for auction. It all sold on the appointed, scheduled day.

My Dad in turn had a pet phrase for me: "I read you like a book; I read you like a book." I treasure that time working with him as ... precious, golden, and holy.

PSALMS 27:1 – The MESSAGE. "Light, space, zest – that's GOD! So, with him on my side I'm fearless, afraid of no one and nothing." Dr. Lester Sumrall declares that Faith is the opposite of all fear: fear of change, fear of people, fear of the unknown, fear of taking on responsibilities, fear of failure, fear of added work, fear of physical or mental breakdown.

"God is about to do something BIG! ... . God is birthing something on the inside of YOU and its coming to FRUITION in this season!!!!!" (Co-Pastor Sheron Strong – Chicago)

"Success" is me commanding mental thoughts of discouragement to flee. Satan knows that there is greatness inside me, and that I am giving GOD my preparation, focus, commitment and patience. I refuse to be discouraged.

My Pastor upon learning that his first name, 'Joseph,' means "God will add" answered my question: "What do you desire God will add ...?" He wrote: "Hmmmm ... I should choose well ..."

> My middle name is 'Joseph.' What will He add to me?
> "With my writing He is going to take me places I never
> dreamed of." Talk about the way you want to be. You
> are prophesying your future. The BIG 'whether' for me
> is: "Will 'Dawn and I' be married within five years?"
> "Have a good day tomorrow." [You, too.]

I like strawberries.

I range from Yoplait strawberry shortcake and strawberry cheesecake yogurts to NutriGrain strawberry snack bars to Oat and Honey Clusters with real strawberries for cereal. As for fresh strawberries I try to stay away from the pesticides. Strawberry shortcake with whipped cream is also a delicacy.

Excerpts from a Trinity Broadcast interview

"Risk, fear, change" are the three major killers of dreams and not maximizing one's Potential. Every great leader has a vision and looks to the horizon. "Character, counsel, leadership" work together for outstanding success.

MATTHEW 6:33 and LUKE 12:31a – The MESSAGE (Both have a same translation). "Steep yourself in God-reality, God-initiative, God-provisions. You'll find all your everyday human concerns will be met. Don't be afraid of missing out."

PROVERBS 27:18 – The MESSAGE. "If you care for your orchard, you'll enjoy its fruit; if you honor your boss, you'll be honored."

"Never be discouraged by the size of your crowd; be fruitful over a few and God will make you a leader of many!" (Pastor Spence – Stockbridge, Georgia)

My crowd of 'Readers' was small, but I kept
writing. I am a powerful soul winner.

REVELATION 12:11 – KJV. "And they overcame him by the blood of the Lamb, and by the word of their testimony; and they loved not their lives unto the death."

Honesty (Dating & Personals)

"Being able to talk through the tough stuff points to a healthy, open relationship for years to come."

[That's what I wanted to hear.]
[Sounds good]

Your re-Baptism and dedication to God on Wednesday September 18, 2013 is equivalent to my 'new birth' (born-again) experience on Saturday 18 December 1971.

How did you come to Christ?

At age of 10 a girl-friend invited me to the Baptist Church. My Mother said I could go. I was the 1st person in my family to come to know the Lord.

Keep "SAYING SO": keep declaring it and God will do it.

I want my words to change the situation. I am healthy. I am prosperous. I have the favor of God. I am strong in the Lord. I am one of a kind. God will add to me … a spouse!!! I have great Clarity in my writings. God is going to show me something that I have never seen. I thank God for His daily Blessings. The right people are in my future. My heart is receptive. With long life God is going to satisfy me. (Inspired by 'Rev. Joel Osteen')

Dawn's reaction to this chapter: [It's all GOOD.]

Who we become in five years depends on the books we read and the people we meet and share with!!! 'Christ' has to be at the center of our life in order for it to be productive. The choices we make will affect our chances to be fruitful. Through the changes that occur daily we face new challenges. It is not necessary to be 100% perfect, only JESUS was 100% perfect. God's grace and mercy provide more than enough eternal safety to all that accept and treasure Him.

Q. How many uses of SALT have you experienced?

A. (1) Seasoning – taste. (2) Preserving. (3) To make thirsty. (4) Buoyancy. (5) Healing. (6) Prevents dehydration. (7) Fire extinguisher. (8) Melts ice.

ECCLESIASTES 9:10 – KJV. "Whatsoever thy hand findeth to do, do it with thy might; for there is no work, nor device, nor knowledge, nor wisdom, in the grave, whither thou goest."

This is the 1st Scripture 'David Green' uses in his book HOBBY LOBBY.

"Read your Bible not in Hebrew, Greek, or English but in the Holy Ghost . . !" (Pastor Simon James)

My illumination from God: "Just as JESUS is Christmas: the Holy Spirit is New Years."

HUGS: "You are so COOL."
[So are you.]

Is there any better compliment / complement than ZECHARIAH 8:23c – KJV. "We will go with you: for we have learned that God is with you"?

Thank you for the encouragement and inspiration.
[It will be.]

Fully Rely on God – 1, 7-15-2014

GOD is always on the alert, constantly on the lookout for people who are totally committed to him. My father 'Albin' was 100% for GOD. My Big Rapids neighbor, 'Isaac French,' (Jim) commented after reading my 1st autobiography "MOMENT-u-M" that I should tell stories with as many details as possible about my experiences, and it would be FUN reading for everybody. Let me start with "3" stories where I trusted my Dad, and he come through for me.

After leaving 'Collegio Americano del Nord,' Vatican City State, on 23 December 1971 because of health reasons, 'Monsignor James P. Moran,' (the Rector at St. Joseph's Seminary) offered the seminary route to my father's discernment, saying: "Ronald could take his exams at the Provincial Seminary in Plymouth, MI." My Dad declined this route for me.

In April 1972 I drove to the Chancery Office in Grand Rapids to meet with 'Bishop Joseph M. Breitenbeck.' We agreed that is would be "a permanent decision not to continue for priesthood for the Grand Rapids diocese."

After beginning to work as 'a male orderly' at Greenridge Nursing Home (now Metron) in October 1973 after seven weeks in the Kent Oaks, Grand Rapids Psychiatric Unit I did not know in advance where I would work starting at 7 a.m. There were east/

west corridors, north/south wings where I could be assigned for the day. In May 1974 I had to take a week to rest and recover because of THE STRESS in working north, west corridor. DAD talked to Management and they agreed to put me on south – usually west corridor. I would give showers to the men and a daily shower to the man who itched his sores.

GOD desired that I live in Bay City / Essexville in the same upstairs apartment with the rent $110 each month from September 1977 to October 1984. This location was halfway between Bay City All Saints north and south campuses. In November 1985 the new owner raised the rent to $125. It was then that my father invited me to work with him in his LAW OFFICES. He and Mom arranged for me to live in the upstairs apartment diagonally across the alley from their home.

PSALMS 13:5-6. [The MESSAGE]. "I've thrown myself headlong into your arms – I'm celebrating your rescue. I'm singing at the top of my lungs, I'm so full of answered prayers."

In 2013 I asked God: "THREE IN ONE, please give me Clarity." Now, a year later, I am thanking God for this 'Clarity' in my writings. His special name is: "God of Wholeness."

My seminary years (10 1/3 years) give me a unique impression of life and God. I was set apart for service to God in a rare, very unusual way. From an early age (for now we will go back to high school) I was trained to be 'a man of Prayer.' I excelled in the classroom and on the athletic courts and fields.

PSALMS 62:1 – The MESSAGE. "God, the one and only – I'll wait as long as he says. Everything I need comes from him, so why not?"

'Jack Findley' (who became a worker for Xerox like my Brother Gary) coached our freshman basketball team. We were humiliated "59-0" on the gridiron in touch football by the sophomore bullies. Some of my classmates bet desserts and were spotted so many points and all lost desserts except for the freshman who received a 60-point spot. 'Al Wahmhoff' wanted to lose weight so he got his wish and lost weight.

'Jack Findley,' II-College, had us practice in January and February after lunch on Sundays. Our gymnasium had three basketball courts and four indoor handball courts. There were two locker rooms with 20 shower heads each and a room to dry towels. I practiced as the starting center. At 6'1" I was the tallest. (Not like 6'7" Bill Glunk from Pittsburgh in my Vatican City class).

On game day 'Jack' had a stocky 5'11" forward play center. I played sparingly and not in the final minutes. We led by eight points with 2 ½ minutes to play. There was no 3-point shooting arc in those days. The sophomores put on an all-court press and scored the last 10 points to win "44-42." I was 'SAD,' considering what might have been. We finally defeated them in "BB" as juniors, the first time we defeated them in any sport (softball, football, basketball, baseball).

If I had to make one complaint to God:

I felt like I was the scapegoat for my first five years at St. Joe's.

Remember, I had no biological sisters and my 1st date was during the Christmas holidays at age 30. The relevant Scripture is LEVITICUS 16:20-30. Do not feel sorry for the goat: it did not have the capacity to take on hurt or guilt from sin. Only JESUS THE CHRIST could and did do that.

Imagine what it would be like to be so different from others that you might be excluded because of it. High school seminary and not four years at B.R.H.S. did that to me.

Because of my Parental upbringing, my U.S.A. and foreign travel, my Mental Health Disability – I have a different story to tell the world.

The K.I.S.S. rule: "Keep it simple, Schinderle."

The 1st girl I ever dated was 'Mary Ellen' from St. John's Parish in Essexville. We attended a Church potluck, and then I invited her to 'The Char Haus' in Bay City during her 1977 Christmas holidays from teaching English and Speech plus guiding the Debate Team in Harbor Beach (high school). Harbor Beach is located on Lake Huron in Michigan's thumb. During the 2 ½ years we shared Friendship I made one visit to Harbor Beach, and when she was at home with her parents we attended the Catholic Byzantine Church in Bay City. She was a two-Mass Sunday organist in Harbor Beach.

Describe one friendship where I am the
teacher and my friend is the student.

There is a 14 year age difference, and I began as his Religion teacher. Neither of us are Roman Catholics today. Craig has a biological daughter and his wife has two biological sons. We both enjoy our sports heritage (University of Michigan versus Ohio State). He is the President of the Saginaw Spirit ice hockey team for youths between the ages of 16 – 20. Our birthdays are one day apart. I always email him first and he responds within 12 hours. He knows the importance of Team chemistry as opposed to having individual stars. We both invest in people. The reason we are teacher – student is because he looks up to me favorably for inspiration.

"Ron. Yes this is very accurate. As a note, I have, and have always had great respect for the values that Ron Schinderle lives by. The values of character, honesty, integrity, empathy are all important in your life. Our friendship is one that passes the test of time. We don't see each other often, but both know that we pray for each other on a regular basis. Our interest in sports is a common denominator and sharing the Iowa – Michigan football game together was a spectacular day. It was Bob Uefor's last broadcast and the stadium was electric as they celebrated his life.

Hope u are well Ron.

Craig"

PSALMS 63:1a – The MESSAGE. "God, you're my God! I can't get enough of you!"

> Reflect on the specific characteristics of rocks
> and how thy describe God's character

In the (OT) certain rocks were grinding stones for grain.

JEREMIAH 23:29 – KJV. "Is not my word like as a fire? saith the LORD; and like a hammer that breaketh the rock in pieces?"

In MATTHEW 7:24-26 we have the wise man building his house on rock, on bedrock. We also have the foolish man building on top soil, that is, sand. We know that when the heavy rains flood the house built on sand it gets washed away (like 'the Brookside

Dairy Freeze' in Big Rapids in September 1986). GOD is our anchor, most dependable, very stable.

In MATTHEW 16:16-18 we have Peter's confession or profession of faith: "You are the Christ, the Son of the living God." And Jesus said: "You are Peter, a little stone, and on the rock of your confession I will build my church." This is God – unchangeable Rock.

In MATTHEW 21:42 Jesus says the stone which the builders rejected has become the chief cornerstone, the anchor for the whole building.

The Mackinaw Bridge (connecting Upper & Lower Michigan)

The construction of the Mackinaw Bridge began on May 7 & 8, 1954 in St. Ignace and Mackinaw City. The Mackinaw Bridge is the longest suspension bridge in the western hemisphere and 5th longest in the world. The length of the suspension bridge (including anchorage) is 8,614 feet. The total length is 26,372 feet. (5,280 feet is a mile). It became open to traffic on November 1, 1957.

I'LL WORSHIP YOU UNDIVIDED

PSALMS 86:15 – The MESSAGE. "But you, O God, are both tender and kind, not easily angered, immense in love, and you never, never quit."

If God and God alone provides ultimate security and comfort, why do you think many turn to him for help only as a last resort? I know God, THE THREE IN ONE, is my Foundational Rock. For me I like to hang out with Jesus and the Holy Spirit. I call the Father, 'Abba.'

'Dawn' said the reason people call on God as a last resort is because: ["They lack faith."]

MATTHEW 5:14. Yes, let your Light shine, as you are a powerful, loving witness for God.

My Army buddy evaluated "Last resort, coming to God."

JOHN 3:19 – KJV. "And this is the condemnation, that light has come into the world, and men loved darkness rather than light, because their deeds were evil." People enjoy living a life of sin. Many wait until the last minute such as a crisis (Stage 4 cancer, given six months to live) (or a prison salvation). If they come to church, the preacher might condemn them.

GOD is Beautiful.

PSALMS 50:1-2. [KJV]. "The mighty God, even the LORD, hath spoken, and called the earth from the rising of the sun unto the going down thereof. (2) Out of Zion, the perfection of beauty, God hath shined."

1ST CHRONICLES 16:29 – KJV. "Give unto the LORD the glory due unto his name: bring an offering, and come before him: worship the LORD in the beauty of holiness."

Comment on 'OVERFLOW':

"Overflow is what God blesses you with beyond your thinking and imagination." (Pastor Elijah – my older spiritual son)

Overflow for me is JESUS' first miracle: the water into wine at the marriage feast at Cana of Galilee. (JOHN 2:1-11)

MALACHI 3:10 – KJV. "Bring thee all the tithes into the storehouse, that there may be meat in mine house, and prove me now herewith, saith the LORD of hosts, if I will not open you the windows of heaven, and pour you out a blessing, that there shall not be room enough to receive it."

NO ONE IS LEFT OUT.
PSALMS 145:17 – The MESSAGE. "Everything God does is right – the trademark on all his works is love." (Pastor Joe said that he likes this Scripture).

"Are you patient enough to do it God's way?"

God is leading you out of here.

ISAIAH 52:12 – The MESSAGE. "But you don't have to be in a hurry. You're not running from anybody! God is leading you out of here, and the God of Israel is also your rear guard."

A little acorn … A majestic Oak: Becoming a person of value.

The 1st born thinks a parent can love only him or her. When his or her parents love little brother or sister, the 1st born thinks love is used up, and that there is less for him or her. How much is there for children to learn!!!

'Irony,' yet serious business:

At my dentist office they have two girls with the same 1st name: One – 'Ebony.' Two – 'Ivory.'

'Paul McCartney and Stevie Wonder' sang "Ebony and Ivory" in the early 1970s.

On a piano the black keys are "ebony" and the white keys are "ivory."

On a chess board the requirements for Team colors are "light and dark."

Always remember those who serve.

A young boy years ago went into an ice cream parlor / diner. He asked the waitress: "How much does a hot fudge sundae cost? She replied, "50 cents." He said he had to count his money. She returned a little impatient as others were waiting for that table. "How much does a dish of plain ice cream cost?" She snapped back, "35 cents." Again the youth replied, "Let me count my money." When she returned, he said that he would have a plain dish of ice cream. He ate the ice cream, paid the cashier and walked out. When the waitress came to clear his table, tears came to her eyes. Next to the empty dish were two nickels and five pennies. Instead of using his "50 cents" for the sundae, he had tipped the waitress "the 15 cents" that would have upgraded his plain ice cream to the hot fudge sundae that he really wanted. He chose to remember those who serve.

PSALMS 56:11 – KJV. "In God have I put my trust: I will not be afraid what man can do unto me."

"Pray and do not give up." This is the meaning of 'Courage.'

My 2ⁿᵈ Florida Vacation

When I flew to Orlando in 2005 from Grand Rapids (GRR) on Wednesday of Holy Week, I had my stopover in the pelting rain in Atlanta. The airplane I was scheduled to complete my flight was "GROUNDED" because it had been hit by lightning. My grey suitcase was left on an open baggage cart, and the rain seeped into my 30-year-old suitcase. My Mother (already in Florida) purchased a new red suitcase for $51 for my return on the following Wednesday.

"Delta Airlines" gave my Brother Gary a voucher
for $75 or $100 to be used within a year.

ISAIAH 48:17 – KJV. "Thus saith the LORD, thy Redeemer, the Holy One of Israel: I am the LORD thy God which teacheth thee to profit, which leadeth thee by the way that thou shouldest go."

'Amy Grant' was born on 25 November 1960 in Augusta, Georgia – the city that hosts the Masters Golf Tournament each April. As a young adult I collected her records and tape cassettes. For Christmas 2006 my Mother bought me Amy's CD, "The Collection." I now have her DVD "Time Again." I was surprised to learn that 'Amy' has four children.

Unconditional Love (Agape Love)

1ST JOHN 4:10-11. [KJV]. "Herein is love, not that we loved God, but that he loved us, and sent his Son to be the propitiation for our sins. (11) Beloved, if God so loved us, we ought also to love one another."

How has 'Dawn' helped me the most?

"Her zest and enthusiasm to make each day a joy!" is the equivalent of my "Facing life each new day with Courage." You must remember I endured on medications 25+ years of 'Chronic Depression' before God healed me of that in October 2011. Dawn's advice of not slumping in a chair has really boosted my self-esteem. She is the 1st female to actively pray out loud with me continually for God's favor in our lives. She does this freely and confidently expecting results. That means we have the prayer of agreement.

Obedience:

Q: "How long have I been a Christian?"

R. "Ever since I was a BOY in the womb of my Mother." My Parents were a Christian family.

Blessings to all my Readers! His favor makes a way before you. Your choices of 'whether' will be Godly decisions.

Humorous:

Bowling: "Ten pins down." (My barber since 1985 – Larry McNeil)

Banking: "It makes sense to me."

'Rebecca St. James' of Sydney, Australia, was born on 26 July 1977. I am blessed with her music, "The Ultimate Collection" and the DVD "aLIVE in Florida." My Dad was born on 26 July 1920.

According to Big Rapids Missionary to Guatemala 'David Beam' the key to 'MISSIONS' is not Capitalism or Money. "It is operating with faith that our Prayers do produce change and improve living conditions, and that the resources are able to be successfully distributed, and the Church thereby grows."

What is my "SAY SO" and also your recommended "SAY SO"?
Yes, GOD is truly Amazing and I love Him!!!!!
Don't stop praying! … It's your lifeline!!
No one is able to put out (extinguish) my
FIRE OF THE HOLY GHOST.

Do you think God could never understand or forgive some of the things you've done? As a result, have you felt you could never feel comfortable in going to Him or in being open about yourself with Him?

What about the woman of LUKE 7:36-50 [KJV]? " …to whom little is forgiven, the same loveth little." And He said to her: "Thy sins are forgiven. Go in peace."

COLOSSIANS 2:14 – The MESSAGE. "Think of it! All sins forgiven, the slate wiped clean, that old arrest warrant canceled and nailed to Christ's cross."

I am asking God to help me teach (word, demeanor, love, faith, integrity) with my life today and each new day as each new day opens up to me.

'Pastor Curtis Strong': "Amen! To God be the
Glory … God bless u Ronald Schinderle."

Whatever GOD gives us will be HIS BEST. "Amen"

JEREMIAH 33:3 – KJV. "Call unto me, and I will answer thee, and shew thee great and mighty things, which thou knowest not."

1ST CHRONICLES 16:10-11. [KJV]. "Glory ye in his holy name; let the heart of them rejoice that seek the LORD. (11) Seek the LORD and his strength, seek his face continually."

ROMANS 14:17 – KJV. "For the kingdom of God is not meat and drink; but righteousness, and peace, and joy in the Holy Ghost."

LUKE 10:20 – KJV. "Not withstanding in this rejoice not, that the spirits are subject unto you; but rather rejoice, because your names are written in heaven."

The camel is the best survivor in the desert.

The only place I saw a live camel was sightseeing the three pyramids at Gizeh (just outside Cairo, Egypt). It was there at the vender's shop that I was offered an alabaster lion at the perfect price, but I didn't want to carry it in my Boy Scout knapsack for 30 days in India.

September 1st – 30th (India – 1970)

I chose to visit INDIA as one of four Catholic seminarians. We, as students, paid 2nd class train fare to ride 1st class on the mail trains. I slept on one of the two upper berths at night. Our itinerary included: United Arab Airlines from Cairo to Bombay with a fuel stop in 130 degree Kuwait; Ahmedabad, Ghandi's birthplace; Jaipur, the Pink City of India; New Delhi – the capital; Agra and the Taj Mahal; Back to the Archbishop's five night hospitality in New Delhi; Amritsar, the Golden Temple of the Sihks; Ambala; Chandigahr, the most modern city in India in 1970; Varanasi and the cremation mats on the Ganges River; Sarnath, the birthplace of Buddhism; a train meal of rice with no silverware; Howrah / Calcutta; Puri; a flight to Hyderabad; the caves of Ellora and Ajunta; bus ride to Jalgaon. No 1ˢᵗ class cabins to Bombay – awake all night. Then as we shopped in Bombay we learned that 'Nasser,' the President of Egypt (1956-1970) had died. We took the midnight flight to Cairo, arriving early a.m. the day after 'Nasser' died. I bought the French newspaper as a souvenir. Three hours later we were on our way to Rome, Italy.

Through 'Children International' I sponsored 'Uttam' from age 12 – 19 ½. He lived near Calcutta.

PHILIPPIANS 1:6 – The MESSAGE. "There has never been the slightest doubt in my mind that the God who started this great work in you would keep at it and bring it to a flourishing finish on the very day Christ Jesus appears."

Part of my healing is choosing the right word or word combinations. That means eliminating negative thinking and instead have positive, encouraging, uplifting thoughts. By doing that I will have valuable input in Kingdom-building. I ask the Holy Spirit to guide my word choices.

What happens when a believer in CHRIST finds himself or herself in a desert?

When this happens one's prayer life appears "dead." Heaven seems like brass. The person prays, but answers are not immediately forthcoming. Maybe she is suffering / rejoicing with a pregnancy and needs some QUIET time. With endurance: persistence and perseverance pay rich dividends; namely, INTIMACY with the Triune God.

2ND CORINTHIANS 4:7 – KJV. "But we have this treasure in earthen vessels, that the excellency of the power may be of God, and not of us."

My Cousin Mark recommended that I enjoy and share JOHN 10:28-30. I am quoting from the (KJV): "And I give unto them eternal life; and they shall never perish, neither shall any man pluck them out of my hand. (29) My Father, which gave them me, is greater than all; and no man is able to pluck them out of my Father's hand. (30) I and my Father are one."

PHILIPPIANS 4:19 – KJV. "But my God shall supply all your need according to his riches in glory by Christ Jesus."

How a man quits smoking:

He puts a Gideon (NT) in his shirt pocket where his cigarettes used to be. When he reaches for a cigarette, he will touch the Bible. That will serve as a powerful reminder. (Pastor Joe)

Twins: a boy and a girl (An instant family)

'Karen Newman,' the Red Wings Anthem Singer, gave birth to a boy and a girl on Friday 22 March 2002. In 1999 she recorded and distributed her CD "Christmas Kiss." The Detroit Red Wings last won 'the Stanley Cup' in 2008 and Karen was continuing to sing the National Anthem.

Pre-Vatican II

October 11, 2012 marked the 50th Anniversary of the Opening of "Vatican II" by Pope John XXIII. On October 11, 1962 I was a sophomore at St. Joseph's Seminary at 600 Burton Street, Grand Rapids. As a freshman we had studied the old Baltimore Catechism. The daily Masses were in Latin. Individual Priests (our Faculty) said private Masses served by one seminarian on the side altars in the east wing of the Chapel. The first three years of high school sat in the north wing. There were no concelebrated Masses in those days.

In 2006 my Mother's first year of "Assisted Living" in Traverse City, Michigan (where my Niece and her husband and family lived) she sent me this FABULOUS birthday card: "For you, Son. I was thinking of you today, when I realized that I haven't told you in a while how wonderful it is to have you for a son … Sometimes, of course, I worry about you, but that's just a natural part of being a parent. More often, I think about how special you are, and how much joy your cheerfulness and willingness to help out have added to my life … I may have criticized you at times, I may have tried at time to change you, but I love you just the way you are … and the way you are makes me very proud." Love & Blessings, Your Mother. Happy birthday.

On my 24th birthday (2-22-1971) 'Pope Paul VI' concelebrated Latin Sunday afternoon Mass in our North American College Chapel. Then he greeted each seminarian in our dining room. I took a picture of my duplicate bridge partner, 'Ron Pytel,' shaking hands with the Pope. Then it was my turn.

"Hockeytown USA" is Detroit, Michigan.

The Detroit Red Wings (NHL) won 'the Stanley Cup' in 1955, 1997 and 1998, 2002, 2008. My Brother Gary celebrated '2008' by buying me "a Detroit Red Wings Stanley Cup Champions red tee-shirt, short-sleeved."

The Muskegon River / Mitchell Creek

'The Muskegon River' flows out of Higgins / Houghton Lakes and travels SW through Evart, Big Rapids, and Muskegon into Lake Michigan. In the 1890s the Muskegon River was home to woodsmen, the logging industry.

West of Big Rapids 'Mitchell Creek' was a productive trout fishing stream in the late 50s and 60s.

In the 1950s and 60s they planted trout in the Community Pool every year for the opening of Trout season on the last Saturday of April. I remember at about age 11 I couldn't wait until the 8 a.m. whistle blew signaling the official start to the season. I spotted a group of trout at the north end of the pool at 7:55, and I couldn't resist offering my bait on my cane pole line. I caught a trout, but the officials made me throw it back in. That was the only fish I caught that morning.

Early in September 2012 four youths from 'Radical Impact Ministries' joined Pastor Joe at the intersection of Mitchell Creek and the Muskegon River and were "Water Baptized." This is the location where 'Trinity Fellowship Evangelical Free Church' traditionally baptizes people.

"The way you handle your gift will determine the level of success that you will have. Keep honing your gift and your gift will keep making room for you. I declare and decree that you will become a hot commodity in high demand." … "Go ahead and praise Him with your gifted self." (Spencer T. O'Neal, affectionately called 'Pastor Spence' by his congregation)

> What have I accomplished knowing that I did
> so only because GOD intervened?

At New Journey Club I was the Team Captain for RELAY FOR LIFE (American Cancer Society) for four years. We raised $341 the year I watched; then $910, $950, $1500, and $1025 during 2007-2010. 'Jo Ann Barrell Spencer' was a major motivator especially in 2009.

"Instead of looking back at the struggles you faced, look forward to the promises God has for your future. He has amazing things in store for you!" (John Hagee Ministries)

PSALMS 28:6-7. [The MESSAGE]. "Blessed be GOD – he heard me praying. He proved he's on my side; I've thrown my lot in with him. Now I'm jumping for joy, and shouting and singing my thanks to him."

> The steps of a righteous man are ordered
> by JESUS, the Spotless Lamb.

Have a Great Day today and an even better day tomorrow.

Children of Light – 1, 7-23-2014

ZECHARIAH 4:10a – KJV. "For who hath despised the day of small things?"

How good you are is important, but equally important and maybe most important is how great you make those around you. This is not confined to athletes. As a Team Player in the workplace values increase as words and actions bring life. In the U.S.A. military: officers look out for their troops and buddies work together.

A Chaplain's Assistant helped turn my life around at an evening mess hall meal and 'Piercing the Darkness questioning' in Stuttgart, West Germany in the summer of 1971. The questioning centered on "Why should 'I' become a Catholic Priest?" I had to make a decision as an adult. Six months later I was out of the seminary and continuing to serve God with my whole being.

[Get a good night's rest.]

PSALMS 85:8 – KJV. "I will hear what God the LORD will speak: for he will speak peace unto his people, and to his saints: but let them not turn again to folly."

ZECHARIAH 4:6b – KJV. "Not by might, nor by power, but by my spirit, saith the LORD of hosts."

Contentment is knowing that 'Pastor Magumba Carlos
W ... ' (Kampala, Uganda) has his copy of my 25 theological
pages (JESUS and THE BIBLE) and is translating for the
improvement / betterment of those who need 'Luganda Bibles.'
"When we say yes to love ... we say hello
to life." (Michael Anderson)

Is your heart transparent like an open book? King David often
poured out his heart to God. PSALMS 51 shares his contrite
heart.

1ST CHRONICLES 17:2 – KJV. "Then Nathan said unto David, Do
all that is in thine heart; for God is with thee."

As 'Pastor Joe' pointed out: there are two kinds of people. (1)
Those who need what you have; and (2) Those who have what
you need (faith, fighting for you and your future).

Happy reading!

GENESIS 1:5 – KJV. "And God called the light Day, and the
darkness he called Night. And the evening and the morning were
the first day."

ROMANS 12:2 – The MESSAGE. "Fix your attention on God.
You'll be changed from the inside out. Readily recognize what
he wants from you, and quickly respond to it. Unlike the culture
around you, always dragging you down to its level of immaturity,
God brings the best out of you, develops well-formed maturity
in you."

"God is going to use EVERYTHING that you have
been through!!!!!" (Pastor Sheron Strong)

According to JOHN 10:27 I claim that I recognize the voice of the Good Shepherd. Yes, I am a sheep and not a goat. All of my sustenance comes from Jesus' careful provision. It does not go well if I wander away from the other sheep, trusting my own devices and human intelligence. I have been 'delusional' in my past as recently as August 2013. For that I ask GOD for forgiveness and more Grace. I thank Him for His Son's death at Calvary to pay my penalty for SIN and for sending me (born-again) an invitation to the Marriage Feast of the Lamb.

Do I, do you, pray before making decisions, even little decisions? These are 'whethers.' What does the guideline say? If I feel comfortable, I go ahead; but if there is even a glimmer of doubt or hesitancy, I back away until my Guide – the Holy Spirit gives me more time and Prayer to resolve the matter. Thank you, God!!

Q. "Should I type this now on my computer?"

R. "Put on a Christian CD on my $43 2001 Sony from K-Mart or a Christian DVD on my free DVD player."

JAMES 3:16-18. [KJV]. "For where envying and strife is, there is confusion and every evil work. (17) But the wisdom that is from above is first pure, then peaceable, gentle, and easy to be intreated, full of mercy and good fruits, without partiality, and without hypocrisy. (18) And the fruit of righteousness is sown in peace of them that make peace."

"Will this make a difference ten years from now?"
"How about for a favorable eternity?"

May you grow More and More like Christ!

Barren no longer: "It's a Boy!"

GENESIS 18:14 – KJV. "Is any thing too hard for the LORD? At the time appointed I will return unto thee, according to the time of life, and Sarah shall have a son." (Isaac)

GENESIS 30:22-24. [KJV]. "And God remembered Rachel, and God hearkened to her, and opened her womb. (23) And she conceived, and bare a son: and said, God hath taken away my reproach: (24) And she called his name Joseph; and said, The LORD shall add to me another son."

EXODUS 2:2 – KJV. "And the (Levite) woman conceived, and bare a son: and when she saw him that he was a goodly child, she hid him three months." (Moses)

JUDGES 13:24 – KJV. "And the woman (the wife of Manoah) bare a son, and called his name Samson: and the child grew, and the LORD blessed him."

1ST SAMUEL 1:20 – KJV. "Wherefore it came to pass, when the time was come about after Hannah had conceived, that she bare a son, and called his name Samuel, saying, Because I have asked him of the LORD."

PSALMS 113:9 – KJV. "He maketh the barren woman to keep house, and to be a joyful mother of children. Praise ye the LORD."

PSALMS 127:3 – KJV. "Lo, children are an heritage of the LORD: and the fruit of the womb is his reward."

PROVERBS 10:1 – KJV. "The proverbs of Solomon. A wise son maketh a glad father: but a foolish son is the heaviness of his mother."

PROVERBS 15:21 – KJV. "Folly is joy to him that is destitute of wisdom: but a man of understanding walketh uprightly."

LUKE 1:7 – KJV. "And they had no child, because that Elisabeth was barren, and they both were now well stricken in years." (John the Baptist)

"Big children," adults – need Continual Prayer (1ST THESSALONIANS 5:17 – KJV, "Pray without ceasing"), work and finances, friendships, nutrition and exercise, recreation and leisure. They also need proper rest and sleep. I call this style of living: 'Balanced.'

Prophetic Dream: Harmonious in Columbus, Ohio

'The Pacific Corridor': My Uncle Jake was a Navy bombardier in the Pacific Corridor in World War II. Because of his accuracy in trial runs he was rewarded with being able to select his own pilot.

Mixed Marriages are those when two different
Faiths come together in Unity in Marriage.

For example: Staunch Roman Catholic + Word of Faith Community

Jewish + Pentecostal, heavy on evangelical

Twin sons born on November 23rd: The family was raised in Brookfield at Elmbrook Church.

Basketball teams: Marquette University
versus University of Wisconsin

1st son is raising two sons. 2nd son is
raising son and younger daughter.

MATTHEW 18:3 – KJV. "And said, Verily I say unto you, Except ye be converted, and become as little children, ye shall not enter into the kingdom of heaven."

MARK 10:15-16. [KJV]. "Verily I say unto you, Whosoever shall not receive the kingdom of God as a little child, he shall not enter therein. (16) And he took them up in his arms, put his hands upon them, and blessed them."

EPHESIANS 6:4 – KJV. "And, ye fathers, provoke not your children to wrath: but bring them up in the nurture and admonition of the Lord."

REVELATION 3:5 – KJV. "He that overcometh (in Sardis), the same shall be clothed in white rainment; and I will not blot out his name out of the book of life, but I will confess his name before my Father, and before his angels."

A leader sizes up what needs to be done and then goes ahead and does it before he or she is told.

> LUKE 10:20 – KJV. "Not withstanding in this rejoice not, that the spirits are subject unto you; but rather rejoice, because your names are written in heaven."

> "Unconditional Love": 'No strings attached'
> 'Dawn' warned: Watch out and avoid ["Gossip"]

JEREMIAH 17:14 – KJV. "Heal me, O LORD, and I shall be healed; save me, and I shall be saved: for thou art my praise."

GENESIS 22:13 – KJV. "And Abraham lifted up his eyes, and looked, and behold behind him a ram caught in a thicket by his horns: and Abraham went and took the ram, and offered him up for a burnt offering in the stead of his son."

GENESIS 33:5 – KJV. "And he (Esau) lifted up his eyes, and saw the women and the children; and said, Who are those with thee? And he (Jacob) said, The children which God hath graciously given thy servant."

> Doing things in your strength is Pride.
> 'Humility' is God-centered.
> You cannot grow without going on with God.
> PROVERBS 1:10 – KJV. "My son, if sinners
> entice thee, consent thou not."
> I am spiritually hungry for more of God. I
> must grow, not stay on the same level.
> When I step up in faith God is there to … pick
> me up. GOD (not the world) blesses me.
> And immediately once we get in the right
> place God will bless obedience.

A very crucial, life-changing 'whether':

After I completed my 'BA degree cum laude' at St. John Vianney Seminary (now Christ the King Seminary) located 12 miles SE of Buffalo, N.Y. there was a decision to be made. On his deathbed 'Bishop Allen J. Babcock' assigned me to Rome for theological studies instead of Plymouth, Michigan (and its 9-hole golf course).

The result of that decision: I became a world traveler. I also won the Men's Golf Championship at Winter's Creek on Sunday September 10, 1972 with my '3-over par,' 38 + 37 = 75.

It is a sunny 78 degree day with fluffy clouds, and our family of four has just settled in for a picnic lunch in Western Canada. Dad had vacated the table in favor of a potential photo of a nearby nature scene. He returned in time to capture on film our picnic table invaded by a black bear. Mom, Gary, and I were safely nestled in our car. Sightseers were enjoying our piece of history. Before Dad entered our car he took a Kodak slide of the picnic table, black bear, and our auto. Back in Big Rapids I received a framed 4" x 4" color photo of this black bear enjoying our cookies and milk.

On that 1962 Monday afternoon Dad phoned his Dad in Iron Mountain. This time Grandpa accepted the collect call. Grandma had passed on to be with the Lord on Sunday afternoon. This ended our leisurely enjoying Canada's Mother Nature in the Province of Alberta. On to Calgary International Airport we sped. 'Albin' caught the next flight to Milwaukee. Mother had us set up our tent / trailer using the airport fence. In the morning Gary and I left our two metal six foot tent poles in the parking lot.

My Niece, 'Kristy,' did the genealogy of our family. Grandpa 'Rudy Schinderle' had one brother and five sisters. His father brought the family name 'Chinderle' from Austria. In America an "S" was added to the original name. Many of Rudolph Schinderle's relatives lived in Milwaukee, and that is where my father was born in 1920. 'Rudy,' however, had settled in the Italian section of Iron Mountain and married 'Clara Arsenault,' a resident of Iron Mountain.

'Grandpa Rudy' and 'Uncle Joe' Arsenault only visited Big Rapids once in my lifetime, and that was after 'Clara' died. They discussed the project of cutting down the box elder tree that was located within five feet of our cement back porch. Many years later the tree was cut down although several branches had been trimmed earlier.

When my Mother was in "Assisted Living" in Traverse City, Michigan, her dietician recommended that she eat three bananas a week to give her a boost of potassium. Now that she is in "Assisted Living" in Big Rapids (since June 30, 2010) she drinks two glasses of milk a day with supplements so that she can remain healthy even though she now has alzheimers disease.

Humorous. God enjoys Major League Baseball games, but perhaps he enjoys bowling even more with its thunder and lightning. "The average change up is 83" mph in MLB.

MATTHEW 13:52 – KJV. "Then said he unto them, Therefore every scribe which is instructed unto the kingdom of heaven is like a man that is an householder, which bringeth forth out of his treasure things new and old."

'Bar mitzvah': a Jewish boy who reaches his 13th birthday and attains the age of religious duty and responsibility *(Webster's Seventh New Collegiate Dictionary)*. JESUS went to the Temple in Jerusalem with his parents at the age of 12.

My right of passage: 6th grade – age 12 (May or June)

My Dad was 5'9" or 5'10" in stature. I reached puberty when my height equaled his shoulder pits. On the cherished weekend we fished the Pere Marquette River near Baldwin for trout. No fish caught. On Sunday we attended the Knights of Columbus breakfast in Ludington before we fished 2-3 hours for anything from the pier. No fish caught. (I later grew to 6'1" in the 9th grade and that was the end of my growth spurt. I was 'lean'; that meant I was neither fat nor bulky.)

7th grade: "The Sacrament of Confirmation"

In the spring of 1960 'Bishop Allen J. Babcock' anointed me and Gary as we each received the Sacrament of Confirmation. 'Bishop Babcock' confirmed the 6th, 7th, and 8th graders in an evening ceremony. My sponsor was the optometrist, 'Dr. Leo Scholler,' the man my Dad recommended. 'Dr. Scholler' gave me a daily Missal to follow the Daily Mass Prayers (a very valuable gift to a potential seminarian). He had a son who attended seminary out-of-state for a couple of years. For my Confirmation name I finally settled on 'Michael,' a name meaning – "Who is like the Lord?"

Fr. Ignatius J. Allen

He taught me how to offer Latin Mass and thereby prepare the new altar boys for service.

Homesickness

When I traveled to the Boy Scout National Jamboree in Colorado Springs, Colorado, in 1960 at the age of 13, my Dad was our Lead Scoutmaster. One of our scouts did get very homesick and my Dad had to travel to Denver to put the youngster (younger than me) on a plane, returning him to his parents in the Grand Rapids area.

At age 14 I left home for 10 1/3 years of seminary. After supper the 1st night I stood by my basement athletic locker and had a GOOD

CRY for 20 minutes. Thereafter, I had no more homesickness. God, my Heavenly Father, took the pain of leaving home away from me. Years later my Mother revealed to me that DAD had a hard time releasing me to God.

"We are praying for you today. You are not alone."

(Bishop Caleb Don Crigger and his wife Brenda)

"Generally speaking"

As a College student at St. Joseph's Seminary I coached the High School Varsity basketball team for two seasons. My repeatable word was "basically." My players caught me using the term often. Today, thinking back, I think the word showed 'indecisiveness.' We played four Varsity games the 1st year and three the 2nd. We played Saginaw Sts. Peter & Paul Seminary each year beginning in 1964 when I was a high school junior. The calendar date was March 19th, the Feast of St. Joseph. Today it is no longer a seminary; it is Saginaw Nouvel High School.

Auto Racing

Jimmie Johnson, #48, Lowe's Car, won the 2013 Daytona 500. My favorite NASCAR driver is 'Matt Kenseth.'

When I was living on Marion Avenue I would listen to the Indianapolis 500 on radio. My favorite winning driver was 'A.J. Foyt.'

A wooden baseball bat: antique!!!

'Grandpa Rudy' gave me this bat while I was in grade school and sleeping upstairs in his attic at the corner of Main & Aragon in Iron Mountain. I have 'Treasured' it for over 50 years. Most wooden bats that I know of come from "Louisville Sluggers." This one is a "Texas Leaguer" from INDIANA BAT CO., PAOLI – IND. It measures 34 inches and is very dark in color with branded lettering.

After nine years in Adult Foster Care (1985-1994), staying that long because I did not want to be responsible for cooking my own meals, I moved into North Parkview Village in September 1994. I began attending the non-denominational Pentecostal church two blocks from my apartment. 'Pastor Jim Austin' and 'Pastor Thomas Pizzo' were the combined "Pastor" of a merged church. Soon thereafter 'Pastor Tom' decided to move up north and continue working at FERRIS.

Three years later (in September 1997) I settled in my present upstairs apartment. The Pastor's wife, 'Mary Austin,' began giving me rides to church. It is a 23 minute walk home from that location, 430 N. Third Avenue.

'Pastor Austin' referred to the "Special Music" after Praise and Worship (before he spoke a lesson for the children) as "dessert without the calories." It was Oh so good! 'Mary Austin' advised: "Read Scripture out loud even when you are at home studying the Word." Satan hates it when the Bible is quoted, quoted in his face and applied to our daily living. Claim its promises. Know your identity in Christ Jesus. Seek out your purpose(s) for life on this Planet. Work towards your Destiny Goals. This is growing in spiritual Maturity.

"I am a Writer."

After church at Christ's Harvest Ministries in the early 2000s a man asked about "the M" on my blue shirt. I told him both my parents graduated from the University of Michigan. "My Dad was a lawyer but he passed on in '86. My Mother was a librarian but she is retired now." He asked further, "Did it pass down to you?" I responded, "I am a writer." To that he said: "How do you make a go of it?" Calmly I replied, "You have to give it to God first." That caught him by surprise and he walked away saying, "I'll have to do that."

Q. "Do you need something recovered?"

R. "A disintegrating marriage; young people that are addicted; accounts receivable; health issues; Peace that passeth all understanding."

Prophecy at REVIVAL PRAYER in 2008:
"Some of you will take nations for Christ."
(People present: Pastor James, Rev. Joe, a foreigner, and me)
'Zeek,' as a fisher of men keep reaching
souls "Till the net is full," my friend.

SPEAK LIFE

The Bible teaches that "money" cannot buy happiness. However, when it is shared with the less Fortunate, the hurting, those that need and require a touch of Love – then it becomes a powerful tool, an instrument for good. When it is given cheerfully and with 'no strings attached,' to share the Gospel locally or in Africa, Central America, South America or the countries of Pakistan,

India, and China, such generosity reaps a multi-fold Harvest of souls for God's Kingdom.

Unity in the Body

There are "regular Joe's" and "average Joe's." Then there is "my Pastor Joe" who is an earthly Mentor led by the Spirit of Love. His preaching goes far deeper than Scripture verse after Scripture verse with the intention of proving his dogma. He is "a Destiny Preacher." That means that his sermons call for application by all who hear them. He believes "Church should be Fun." Every Sunday and Tuesday night is different as led by the Holy Spirit. He often takes off without sermon notes, using his "Power Bible" on his computer. We believe the Word of God (the Bible) is inerrant and the Ultimate Authority. Yes, there is Freedom in the Spirit at "Radical Impact Ministries." All is done 'decently' and 'in proper order.'

My spiritual eyes are focused and fixed on "Destiny Goals." Reaching people wherever they are with THE GOOD NEWS is primary for me.

The book of REVELATION: We and the Lamb
are "the Salvation – Glory Message."

PROVERBS 14:25 – KJV. "A true witness delivereth souls: but a deceitful witness speaketh lies."

When the Master Shows Up:

LUKE 12:48 – The MESSAGE. "Great gifts mean great responsibilities; greater gifts, greater responsibilities."

"We cannot love a person we do not know, and we cannot know a person to whom we have not listened." (REJOICE IN ME, Monsignor David E. Rosage)

My Mother and I spent a Saturday together in Grand Rapids at the old St. Joseph's Seminary. We listened to 'Monsignor Rosage' as he shared in the Chapel. We arrived safely in Big Rapids just in time for supper at Big Boy Restaurant. As I was leaving "Big Boy" I found $5 in the entranceway.

My closest friend at the North American College 'Fr.' Bob Striegel from Iowa sowed into the Kingdom a month and a half to Kenya / Uganda as "a Deacon." I sent him money to buy African souvenirs for me. He found a black lion with three ivory teeth, but these teeth have long ago fallen out. He also sent me an African male riding 'a water buffalo.' It measured 6 ¾ inches at its base and 8" from the bottom to the tip of the rider's hat (protecting him from the sun).

I gave the water buffalo to 'Ann Cottle' at Peter McHugh's Prayer Time in January 2013 for her birthday.

PROVERBS 3:35 – KJV. "The wise shall inherit glory: but shame shall be the promotion of fools."

"Money" does not get you into heaven. God is not for sale. When you sow continuously into the work of the Ministry your reward in heaven is a Treasure you could not fathom while living on earth. Be generous with a loving heart. Live for God; not for the world.

> The story of 'Boaz' is a redemption story,
> not a Valentine story. (Pastor Joe)

A fresh anointing of joy for 'Dawn' with a
promotion of peace, taken to the next level!

Every life has Purpose.

For 'the Newcomer': Decide today, tonight, to tap into the grace of God that will cause healing and deliverance which are inseparable; leading to victory in every area of your life. God (Abba, Father) patiently waits for you to make that decision for him.

Exhortation from 'Michele Michi Gallaudet
Willison' of Shiloh Pines:
"Keep your eyes on Jesus, and do whatever He tells you to do."
Ronald loves God and expects Him to
be dynamic each new day!

Prosperity in the Greek means "to have a good journey."
Life is a journey!

From my Cousin Mark in Michigan's U.P.: "Keep praying for my two boys. When we love JESUS with all our hearts, mind, and strength – everything else takes care of itself."

Do you celebrate Christmas in Andhra Pradesh, India?

"JESUS is shared in Love. That is much more important than decorations, gifts, and food. Christmas is a celebration of God's Love for mankind. JESUS IS OUR SAVIOR. That is the truest meaning of Christmas."

I believe my success story of "Courage over Chronic Depression and Schizophrenia" is a living Testimony of God working within me. "I am on Fire for God." The Holy Spirit lives within me. In

2010 on a Wednesday night at Shiloh Pines I saw 'deep colors' vividly for the 1st time in memory.

"You're beautiful! Very beautiful!!"
[I appreciate that.]

[Be careful.]
"What do you want me to be careful about?"
[LIFE]

ABBA – 1

[Sweet dreams]

Almost all Americans are or have been or will be married. The future according to 'Dawn' is for hope and for dreams to come true.

Facebook photo: "Pray not because you need something but because you have a lot to thank God for!"

On Saturday 9 August 2014 I read: "The thought idol in my mind is equal to my hand idol." In the morning at 8:40 I woke up saying, "I've got our wedding cake all baked." Yes, in the flesh I am a 'nobody.' However, in the spirit I am 'Sir Ronald, the Knight of the Word.'

Have a pleasant, prosperous, healthy day!
[Happy Day]

'Kathy R' has two Scriptures that she holds firm. NEHEMIAH 8:10c – "The joy of the Lord is my strength" and PHILIPPIANS 4:13 – "I can do all things through Christ who strengthens me."

'Darren' defines joy: "The abundance of
His Presence with perfect Peace."

His Scripture is ECCLESIASTES 2:26.

'Pastor Joe' likes the reign of Jehoshaphat. His Scripture is 2ND CHRONICLES 20:20b-21.

On Sunday 10 August 2014 'Rev. Joseph N. Cottle' exhorted: Pray!!!!! "Next step" – pray a loud in your Holy Spirit prayer language whether that be in English or in Tongues.

On Sunday 10 August I had a new "WHETHER." Will I type my book story on a Sunday or will I wait until Monday like I did for all the pages of my 1st half. This temptation was to change my boundaries. I am glad I waited and did extra praying.

In May 2012 I made two 22" x 28" collages. In the bottom right corner of both "prayer boards" I had a mother and daughter in a bathroom ad from Lowe's. In March 2013 and 2014 I celebrated Dawn's birthday. Her life or death Scripture is: "Casting all your care upon him; for he careth for you." (1ST PETER 5:7 – KJV)

I did not become a Catholic Priest or a Catholic Deacon, but the call to follow JESUS is a universal call to all people!!!!

ESTHER 4:14 – The place where you are at in life might be exactly where you need to be "for such a time as this."

The secret that distinguishes professional writing from that of 'the average Slim Jim or the average Joe' is given us by KODAK: *"The genius is in the details."* My Dad had a square Kodak camera that took 12 slides on his Extachrome 127 film.

How do I praise God cheerfully?

"I look at crisis as a divine indication of growth, that something needs to be adjusted, or as a divine announcement that heaven is ready to birth something new into my life. All I need to do is adjust my mindset, alter the decisions I make and the options I choose every day.

"Pain does not always equate with something bad; it could simply mean it's time to adjust. It could be an indication that the time has passed for you to be where you are now and that you need to push to the next level.

"You must be able to clear your mind and heart of what you feel is the main reason for your struggles or your pain and look beyond to ask whether God is pushing you into a position where He can reveal His purpose for the earth through you." (Ellaine is Mbali's twin, my spiritual daughters near Durban, South Africa.}

Happy people are full of gratitude!!

I thank ABBA for a healthy heart, a God-filled brain, an immortal soul (mind, will, and emotions), for caring friends, That the sunshine appears on my western balcony, for people who give me automobile rides, for my family and extended family, for ROZES.

'Joy' is a Holy Spirit fruit as 'Tongues' are a Holy Spirit gift.

"Every transformation takes time." (Bishop T.D. Jakes)

God is the author of Wisdom. He is all-knowing, everywhere present at the same time, and consistently all-loving. He sent to Planet Earth His only-begotten Son to pay the price of SIN as the

2nd Adam. JESUS (Yeshua) is the Christ, the Anointed One, the true Messiah. Born in the city of David (Beth-lehem), six miles south of Jerusalem, He is the living Word of God.

"What do you do when God has you in a holding pattern?" (Bishop T.D. Jakes)

HEBREWS 11:6 – KJV. "But without faith it is impossible to please him: for he that cometh to God must believe that he is, and that he is a rewarder of them that diligently seek him."

Morning Prayer

Good morning, GOD. Good morning, Heavenly Father. Good morning, Heavenly Father. I love You, dear Jesus. I love You, dear Jesus. I love You, dear Jesus. Thank You for creating me. Thank You for creating 'Dawn.' Thank You for creating me. Thank You for creating 'Dawn.' Thank You for creating me. Thank You for creating 'Dawn.'

"In the morning I shall look up." From crystal chandelier to the framed postage stamp 'Bird Watching' picture ($35 at MCMC in the autumn of 2012) … to green shaded oak leaves.

Ahha

In the Hebrew the word for 'man' is very close to the word for 'woman.'

Y H W H: 'Yahweh' in the Jerusalem Bible. 'Jehovah' for … many other people.

'Abram' had his name changed to "Abraham – meaning: the Father of many nations." Sarai his wife had her named changed to 'Sarah.' HA and AH mean LIFE in Hebrew.

'Theresa' is either changed to 'Teresa' or 'Teresah.'

According to 'Alice': "There aren't many books written by Catholics."

Exhortation to Unity: Repent. The
Scripture is Ephesians 4:11-13.

EPHESIANS 4:11-13. [KJV]. "And he gave some, apostles; and some, prophets; and some, evangelists; and some, pastors and teachers; (12) For the perfecting of the saints, for the work of the ministry, for the edifying of the body of Christ: (13) Till we all come in the unity of the faith, and of the knowledge of the Son of God, unto a perfect man, unto the measure of the stature of the fullness of Christ:."

The Prayer of Jabez => 1ST CHRONICLES 4:9-10
"O God, I do not want to settle for too little from you."

HEBREWS 11:6b. GOD is a rewarder of those who diligently seek Him. Fully rely on God to bless you and yours! When Charter Communications (Charter Spectrum) went HD my Brother Gary bought me a 42 inch HD Haier TV. When Windows XP eliminated itself, my Brother bought me a Windows 7, Microsoft Office 2013 computer tower and paid for lessons for me to learn how to use it. When 'Dawn' sold her chocolate brown davenport my Brother helped me buy it as a 2013 Christmas present. GOD has richly blessed my Brother and his wife of 43 years. I am really really grateful.

Jabez and Ronald

1ST CHRONICLES 4:9-10. [KJV]. "And Jabez was more honourable than his brethren: and his mother called his name Jabez, saying, Because I bare him with sorrow. (10) And Jabez called on the God of Israel, saying, Oh that thou wouldest bless me indeed, and enlarge my coast, and that thine hand might be with me, and that thou wouldest keep me from evil, that it may not grieve me! And God granted him that which he requested."

Jabez and Ronald called on the God of Israel: Bless us indeed. Enlarge our territory. Keep us from temptations that we will not cause pain. Help us smile and be generous givers, that others will embrace the Christ – our Savior, Messiah and Lord.

PSALMS 103:2-3. [KJV]. "Bless the LORD, O my soul, and forget not all his benefits: (3) Who forgiveth all thine iniquities; who healeth all thy diseases;."

"You can shrink in number … and grow in power."
(Minister Dr. Rod Parsley – Columbus, Ohio.)

This happened to 'Radical Impact Ministries Motivational & Media' (RIMMM): From Shiloh Pines Retreat House in 2010 to Isabella Bank Conference Room, to the Holiday Inn Auditorium and swimming pool for 'Water Baptisms.' Then on to Pepper's Café and Deli, Austin Township Hall east of Stanwood, Aetna Township Hall in Morley to Pastor Joe's garage in the summer of 2014.

How do I praise God cheerfully? I use "The MESSAGE" by 'Eugene H. Peterson' as my modern American English Bible and the King James Version (KJV) as my standard text. My sample from The MESSAGE is PHILIPPIANS 4:6a, 7b. "Don't fret or worry instead of worry, pray … It's wonderful what happens when Christ displaces worry at the center of your life."

Be blessed as only our loving Heavenly Father can bless.

My assignment, our assignment, is to give 'Abba' glory.

The Truth about me is always what God says! Not what I think or feel; not what others say, think or do. The truest thing about me is what God says!" 'Abba' says in his Word that I am "chosen, forgiven, restored, redeemed, valuable, a Masterpiece."

Increase: not 100% which is double. 'The barley harvest' is Passover time. 'The wheat harvest' is Pentecost time. 'The corn harvest' becomes 30-fold as drought sets in. However, 'the corn harvest' with ideal weather (some soaking rain) is 60-fold and in Nebraska, 100-fold.

My 1st and only CHILDREN'S BIBLE was a collection of Haiku poems, a natural and a supernatural birth, and … and not a Caesarean birth although the baby got caught in the birth canal for '4' hours and the mother actually was so weak with her 7.2 pound baby that she could not (was not allowed to) hold 'A.B.C.'

Are you superstitious?

In Japan "4" is unlucky. Therefore, golf balls are manufactured #1, #2, #3, and #7. Perhaps that is why 'the Emperor' attacked "Pearl Harbor, Hawaii" on 12/7 – a Sunday.

Successful Prayer

JAMES 5:13-15. [The MESSAGE]. "Are you hurting? Pray. Do you feel great? Sing. Are you sick? Call the church leaders together to pray and anoint you with oil in the name of the Master. Believing prayer will heal you, and Jesus will put you on your feet. And if you've sinned, you'll be forgiven – healed inside and out."

"What God is giving you requires preparation, focus, commitment and patience. Discouragement is the enemy's favorite tool against you. He knows there is greatness inside you. Kick the devil in the teeth. Don't give up." (Daystar Television Network)

Depression is getting stuck in yesterdays. My daily declarations to the Lord, my SAY SO, will help me reach my Destiny Goals, complete my earthly assignments, and ... be prepared for the Marriage Feast of the Lamb.

Do not settle 4 less than "The Best."

1ST PETER 1:2b – The MESSAGE. "May everything good from God be yours."

The deeper the assignment the more intense the preparation.

PSALMS 45:1c – KJV. ": my tongue is the pen of a ready writer." PSALMS 48:1-2. [KJV]. "Great is the LORD, and greatly to be praised in the city of our God, in the mountain of his holiness. (2) Beautiful for situation, the joy of the whole earth, is Mount Zion, on the sides of the north, the city of the great King."

How might two people live? Richly blessed. Dawn sows 'love.' I sow 'mercy.' These are seeds in the Kingdom for Jesus, our Savior King.

Prince Charles and Lady Diana's 1st born, Prince William, married Catherine Middleton on the Anglican feast of St. Catherine of Siena. 'Kate' is now the Duchess of Cambridge. Her 1st born is in line to become King George. Her 2nd baby is due in April 2015.

Music on [JCTV]

"6, r, 4, 3, 2, 1 – Everybody go wild."

Art thou ready for thy Water Baptism?

The prayer for 'Repentance' – "Re-dedication" is found in ROMANS 10:9-10.

'Trustworthy' is one the Boy Scout's 12 Laws.

Where do you draw your adult faith from? It took me 24 years to confess "The Lord is Jesus the Christ, the Anointed One." That was 18 December 1971.

Open the door, my friend.

Stocky, husky, brawny: I was not 'a fat dude' when I played 6th grade tackle football.

I was lean and lanky in September 1972 when I won the Men's Golf Championship at Winter's Creek Golf Course. My score that day was: "38 + 37 = 75." I had three birdies and one "OB."

Thanksgiving is … giving GOD the best return on His goodness.

PSALMS 20:6 – The MESSAGE. "That clinches it – help's coming, an answer's on the way, everything's going to work out."

"Give your faith some action, you will be
surprised at the results." (Pastor Joe)

In 2003 courtesy of the Salvation Army I watched my 1st Detroit Tigers game at Comerica Park. It was game #159, and the play-off bound Minnesota Twins were in town. That Friday night it started to rain in the 9th inning, and we headed out of the stadium in a tie-game. In the 10th Minnesota gave Detroit its 119th loss. A season with only 43 wins is a culture changer. Catcher Ivan Rodriguez signed a free agent contract and played 2004-2007 plus part of 2008. Detroit became competitive and played in the 2006 World Series against the St. Louis Cardinals.

Give your faith some action: you'll be surprised at the results.

"Christmas 2009" became my seventh and final 'Traverse
City Christmas.' On June 30, 2010 'Two Men and a
Truck' moved my Mother to Big Rapids Assisted Living.
My Niece Kristy and her husband decided at that time
to move out of the snow and ice in hopes of finding an
even more fulfilling life. The right business opportunities
brought them to North Carolina and then South Carolina
(Charleston) as they spent a year moving and living in
rented houses. Their "God-move" ended up where son 'Seth'
had boldly declared months earlier: "This is our house."
"Call me if you need anything." (Gary)

DAY

PSALMS 50:10 – KJV. "For every beast of the forest is mine, and the cattle upon a thousand hills."

PSALMS 84:10 – KJV. "For a day in thy courts is better than a thousand. I had rather be a doorkeeper in the house of God, than to dwell in the tents of wickedness."

PSALMS 90:4 – KJV. "For a thousand years in thy sight are but as yesterday when it is past, and as a watch in the night."

In blazing direct sunlight I determined that I, RJS, received the Baptism of the Holy Spirit in the early winter of 1979 in November.

What was Darren's assignment? To integrate (combine) and compile a prayer expressing PSALMS 103 and 139.

"Ein Kinder Gootus (child of God) sprecken de Deutsche?" "If we had not intervened, we would all be speaking German today." (US Air Force Chief Master Sergeant, Mark S. Brejcha)

Biblically, the number "*8*" represents "New Beginnings."

I recently learned "blue" is COLD on one side of a $60 faucet and "red" is HOT on the other side of that female faucet.

What do I put my trust in?

In ISAIAH 31:1-3 many relied on horses and chariots and paid no attention to The Holy of Israel, the One true God. Do any of us rely on automobiles and / or motorcycles and neglect GOD? How about relying on alcohol, tobacco, street drugs? Personally, I enjoy Detroit Tigers baseball. On Friday 22 August 2014 the final score was "Detroit 6 - Twins 20."

MATTHEW 5:33a, 37b – The MESSAGE. "And don't say anything you don't mean." … "Just say 'yes' and 'no.' When you manipulate words to get your own way, you go wrong."

REVIVAL: "3" ingredients.

"Prophecy, Evangelism, and MMuch Love."

"Time, Resources, and Holiness."

"Commitment to the Cause of Jesus!"

Selfishness is the spirit of self-preservation. (Kathy R.)

Always remember those who serve.

1ST PETER 3:4 – KJV. "But let it be the hidden man of the heart, in that which is not corruptible, even the ornament of a meek and quiet spirit, which is in the sight of God of great price."

PSALMS 84:11 – KJV. "For the LORD God is a sun and shield: the LORD will give grace and glory: no good thing will be withheld from them that walk uprightly."

In Michigan winter each new day has the potential for rain, freezing rain, ice, snow. SUNSHINE.

"Suddenly," "abruptly."

Lower Michigan has two more weeks of summer, then get ready for our autumn color tours as the leaves motivate our attention to "Thank Abba" for His gift of colors.

Every 'either – or' is a WHETHER decision.

What happens after Breakthrough?

My life with Christ (Christ centeredness) becomes the reality. God is not a giant sugar Daddy. We come to Him with the cares of this world and He is #Unstoppable. He has our higher, highest intimacy with Him in mind. He wants us to reach out to Him with Love and the ultimate respect. When we do that over time His reward(s) are out of this world.

> Dr. Sumrall encouraged us: "Be a better person today
> than you were yesterday. Be more mature in your
> Christian walk this week than you were last week."
> "Faith is simply knowing God!" (Pastor Rod
> Parsley summarizing Dr. Lester Sumrall)

MATTHEW 7:13-14. [The MESSAGE]. "Don't look for shortcuts to God. The market is flooded with surefire, easygoing formulas for a successful life that can be preached in your spare time. Don't fall for that stuff, even though crowds of people do. The way to life – to God! – is vigorous and requires total attention."

> In Jesus' name let there be … healing,
> deliverance, financial prosperity.

What is faith? It is positively described in HEBREWS, chapter 11.

Faith is our response to what God has said or done.

Faith must be born in the spirit of man before it is effective.

> 1ST TIMOTHY 6:6 – KJV. "But godliness
> with contentment is great gain."

PSALMS 26:7 – KJV. "That I may publish with the voice of thanksgiving, and tell of all thy wondrous works."

Church History:

"This Season … Your ministry shall begin to grow." (Prophetess C. Makhuvele)

"This is the Season of the Fruit." (Missionary Bonita Bush – South Dakota)

God is Good. God is Great. We thank Him for His goods. We thank Him for His very good gifts. He is Worthy. He is very Worthy. He is worthy of our Praise. Praise Him. Praise Him. PRAISE HYMN.

Holiness

The opposite of WORSHIP is worry. When you worry, you take your focus off God and give false hope to yourself. When you Worship, you focus on Him with all your body, soul, and spirit. On Earth 24 hours each day and 168 hours each week seems significant, but really – compared to eternity with God, time is endless.

A condensed, mini-presentation of the Gospel of Salvation

ACTS 26:18 – KJV. "To open their eyes, and to turn them from darkness to light, and from the power of Satan unto God, that they may receive forgiveness of sins, and inheritance among them which are sanctified by faith that is in me."

In the Old Testament GOD protected Abram, Ishmael, Moses, and Joshua. They fulfilled their assigned duties with God's help. Faith made their jobs do-able. In the New Testament GOD was always there to comfort those who believed JESUS and served God.

> The more I respect and honor my Pastor, the
> closer I will be to God's blessings.

The returning heroes of World War II on the African and European Fronts: they lived words like Honor, Courage, Duty, Sacrifice.

Add + venture forth with CHRIST = 'new experiences.'

Leave behind all unforgiveness, anger, bitterness, and self-pity. This is how we navigate the storms of life whether they are relational, financial, physical. Do not lose faith and hope. GOD says at every season of my life He will be on my side. (Sunday 24 August 2014 – Rev. Stanski)

Everything with a Place and a Purpose

PROVERBS 16:3 – KJV. "Commit thy works unto the LORD, and thy thoughts shall be established."

PROVERBS 16:3 – The MESSAGE. "Put GOD in charge of your work, then what you've planned will take place."

"Love, love, love … Tender love is the secret. Love those you are training. Love those with whom you work. Love those who serve you. Keep this thought in mind: GOD IS LOVE." (Bishop Caleb Don Crigger)

[You are human.]
[Talk to you soon.]

"The Body has many members, all are important
to God. Gratefully yours, RJS."

Intercessory Prayer is with words to God. The Prayer of Intimacy is relaxing in the presence of God. When heart speaks to His heart … with reverence, Love, and gratitude we are at a Time of Worship.

"Love will FIND A WAY," sung by Amy Grant in 'The Collection,' 1986.

I take comfort from Chris Tomlin's 2013 lyrics: "The God of Angel Armies is always by my side."

When 'General Robert E. Lee' of the Confederacy yielded to 'U.S. Grant,' then a Union General, "Lee surrendered all." JESUS surrendered all when he died on the wooden cross at Calvary, just outside the city of Jerusalem.

"Our Father who art in heaven – Abba. Our Father who art in heaven – Abba. Our Father is ABBA."

'Francesca' and 'Patrizia' were … semi-popular Italian youths at "L'oratorio" in Trastevere, Roma, where the boys never took an 'angolo' (corner kick in anticipation of U.S.A. 2 – Ghana 1 in Brazil's 2014 World Cup).

My nickname at the Youth Center was 'Padre Fungo.' I was 6'1" and 145 pounds.

Saint Irenaeus, early 2nd century, praised God: "The glory of God is man fully alive." Is 'my Pontiac' running on all eight cylinders? To better utilize my desk top computer 'Dawn' introduced me to "Spotify" in order to listen to Music: favorite artists, favorite songs. My choice of Music plays in the background while I do other computer functions. It is also the way to load a MP-3 Player for choice music while I exercise, walking!!!

"Fully alive": This challenges me to be a good knight of the Word, selecting Scripture passages and testifying about them.

"Fully alive" has me living written and spoken words in order to build up the body of Christ in the church and in the world.

"Fully alive" challenges my manhood to live holy in the sight of my peers and those that need Christ.

2ND TIMOTHY 2:15 – KJV. "Study to shew thyself approved unto God, a workman that needeth not to be ashamed, rightly dividing the word of truth."

2ND TIMOTHY 3:16 – The MESSAGE. "Every part of Scripture is God-breathed and useful one way or another – showing us truth, exposing our rebellion, correcting our mistakes, training us to live God's way."

My Pastor nicknamed me: "Ronaldus Magnus" (Latin for 'Ronald the Great'). At the Gregorian University I received a grade of '8.5' for my ten minute dialogue talking about "the role of the Laity" in the Roman Catholic Church, Vatican II document. Next in line my very good friend, Edward from Brooklyn told our kind Professor the human limitations of 'Papal Infallibility.' LOL.

The following semester (III – Theology) we had an Italian textbook not translated into English for the class "Faith / Hope." Having read only five pages of this text when I made my Adult profession of Faith in St. Peter's Basilica on Saturday 18 December 1971 as the class ahead of mine were ordained 'Priests' I soon suffered the beginning of a nervous breakdown, suffering from stress, stress, stress because I started to fear passing the exam for that course in late-January 1972. Within a week of my born-again experience in St. Peter's I was home with my Parents and no longer studying for Catholic priesthood.

'Semper fiat': Latin for "Always, thy Will be done."

'Semper fidelis': "Faith Always" starts my day.

Memory Lane: A Testimony from Arlene
(mother of three children)

Arlene attended St. John's Prayer Group in Essexville in 1981 and testified: "You and the prayer group have opened my eyes to God's great love. I am now hearing with different ears." Her 1st born and only daughter, Linda, was born at six months with deafness. Linda is now a cardiologist, and her daughter studied to become a veterinarian. This testimony shows the Goodness of ABBA in the life of my friend.

Church History

"Textbooks": I studied four semesters of Church History at St. John Vianney Seminary in East Aurora, N.Y. (12 miles SE of Buffalo). As a 2nd Semester College Senior my Professor mercifully gave me a "B minus" even though I deserved a "C." As he pointed out: at that time I showed no analytical ability whatsoever. The higher grade helped me rank #4 in our graduating class of "33."

In 1989 (SJV) had become 'Christ the King Seminary' relocated from Olean, N.Y. and St. Bonaventure University. Our youngest and brightest student, Alfons, had become the Dean of Students at this renewed seminary.

"A city rich in history and powerful": in Rome, Italy (living on Vatican State property) I had "2722 years of live history all around me." Even Day 3 in Italy had valuable newness: Sunday Mass in the catacombs. St. Peter's Basilica has over "450 years" of Papal history to share with thousands weekly. Its High Altar is above the tomb of St. Peter, Apostle and 1st Pope.

Do I hold any grudges?

Following a luncheon with 'Father Lam T. Le' in 2008 at a Big Rapids Restaurant he asked me on our drive to my apartment: "Do I hold or harbor a grudge against the Catholic Church or against my Parents?" I now realize I am a product of a flawed system. I am like the clay of JEREMIAH 18:1-6 being reformed by the Potter. I now have become a very useful and very valuable instrument to reach souls for Christ. In truth: "I am a member of the Harvest Generation."

MATTHEW 13:52 – KJV. "Then said he unto them, Therefore every scribe which is instructed unto the kingdom of heaven is like unto a man that is an householder, which bringeth forth out of his treasure things new and old."

From Spencer T. O'Neal: "Transparency is what the Body of Christ needs most in this day and time. Share about where you've been and what you've been through and how your faith pulled you through that process." Echo. Amen.

I left home (Big Rapids) as a 14-year-old and was only homesick for a 20 minute cry after my 1st seminary supper. Then I thanked GOD for this opportunity to start living my calling, and it was 10 1/3 years later that I made my 1st Adult profession of faith. During those seminary years I was a "B" student in high school and a "cum laude" State of New York "Batchelor of Arts" degree recipient at the end of four years of College. My 2 1/3 years of graduate study at the North American College turned me into a world explorer through travel and no academic degree.

When I took a psychological exam as a high school senior, I failed the initial testing. Because my faith was so strong I was allowed to go through counseling, then re-tested, and my seminary days lasted another seven years before I experienced the beginning of a nervous breakdown due to STRESS, STRESS, and greater STRESS.

Socially, I developed very slowly. I have a younger Brother and no sibling sisters. My co-ed College days were at Aquinas College in Grand Rapids as a sophomore living at St. Joseph's Seminary. I did not go on an unchaperoned date until Bay City / Essexville at age 30. Then there was a General Motors secretary in Saginaw that I met as the House of Praise secretary for Rev. Ross Lakes in west-side Bay City in 1983-1984.

After moving from Adult Foster Care to Independent Living in September 1994 people began appearing out of nowhere. On September 26, 1997 I moved to this apartment also in Big

Rapids. In 2001 I dated a woman for 11 months, but we were not compatible for Marriage although we have remained "Friends."

Now there is 'Dawn.' The Whether Question is whether we will get married in the future. My Pastor challenged me: "Am I willing to WAIT and do it God's way?" For now we are enjoying the bonding that is created as Time increases our awareness of each other.

A reminder: Be doubly careful how you speak and act. Your words change the atmosphere.

"Love waits; lust doesn't."
"Time is a weapon God has given us to search out the Truth." (Pastor Joe)

What does it mean to 'thrive'?

According to *Webster's Seventh New Collegiate Dictionary* "thrive" means 'to flourish, prosper, and to progress toward or realize a goal.'

I repaid my unofficial debt to the Grand Rapids diocese by authoring "The Centennial History of St. Mary's Parish, 1873-1973." It was included in the 1973 Centennial Brochure with a Library of Congress number. The Parish sold the brochure for $3.

I agree with Dr. Mike Murdock and The Wisdom Center in Fort Worth, Texas. He teaches that the tithe does not have to be money. He suggests sowing seeds and naming them, seeds such as Time, wisdom, love, patience, and / or money. Abraham tithed a tenth to Melchizedek, the king and priest of Salem (later named 'Jerusalem').

Living a victorious life

PSALMS 19:14 – KJV. "Let the words of my mouth, and the meditation of my heart, be acceptable in thy sight, O LORD, my strength, and my redeemer."

MATTHEW 4:4 – KJV. "But he answered and said, It is written, Man shall not live by bread alone, but by every word that proceedeth out of the mouth of God." (cf. DEUTERONOMY 8:3b)

EPHESIANS 3:20 – The MESSAGE. "God can do anything, you know – far more than you could ever imagine or guess in your wildest dreams! He does it not by pushing us around but by working within us, his Spirit deeply and gently within us."

Freely given: A blessing as a gift
Friendship ring – [If I found someone else,
would you be happy for me?]

PROVERBS 11:30 – KJV. "The fruit of the righteous is
a tree of life; and he that winneth souls is wise."

ISAIAH 64:4 – The MESSAGE. "Since before time began no one has ever imagined, No ear heard, no eye seen, a God like you who works for those who wait for him."

"Draggin' the line" is 'working every day.' From the song writer of "Crimson & Clover."

When I sow 'mercy' …

MATTHEW 5:7 – The MESSAGE. "You're blessed when you care. At the moment of being 'care-full,' you find yourselves cared for."

"Having an understanding heart is one of the beautiful characteristics of mercy." (Joyce Meyer Ministries)

From the Holy Spirit: "I forgave you the first time you asked me."

A little small talk … could lead to a walk on a dirt path where two souls share male / female respect and honor each other.

Answer for yourself: "What foundation is your life built on?"

Beauty within. Created in the image and likeness of God. My name is written in the Lamb's book of life.

I rely on 'Abba,' Jesus our Savior – Lord – King of kings, and the power of the Holy Spirit that accomplishes great things. It is not my strength or wisdom: my weakness reveals God's strength. The ultimate glory goes to Him. I choose to stay full of joy.

"Repent, for the Kingdom of heaven is near. Choose right, choose Christ."

'Elaine' is "Shining Light" in English. Her Zulu name, 'Hlengiwe,' means "Saved – Redeemed."

'Ronald' is "Wise Ruler." 'Joseph' is "God will add … " 'Chinderle' is my Austrian family name; it is generational because of the dimple on my chin.

GRATITUDE is 'my giving thanks to the Almighty.'

"Christ is indeed my Solid Rock and firm foundation." (Ellaine)
Zulu names in South Africa: Hlengwa – xy. Hlengiwa – xx.
"Lets keep the fire burning" PENTECOST comes to Durban!!

JESUS and THE BIBLE, 25 pages translated into 'Urdu' for Islamic Pakistan.

PSALMS 100:4-5. [KJV]. "Enter his gates with thanksgiving, and into his courts with praise: be thankful unto him, and bless his name. (5) For the LORD is good; his mercy is everlasting; and his truth (the Bible) endureth to all generations."

The two great commandments: (1) Love God with all you've got; and (2) Love thy neighbor as thyself. Then MATTHEW 22:40 – KJV continues: "On these two commandments hang all the law and the prophets." Is this where "GRACE," God's unmerited Favor becomes most effective?

Do not forget about the complete Salvation
package: forgiven, healed, delivered.

HEBREWS 12:28-29. [KJV]. "Wherefore we receiving a kingdom which cannot be moved, let us have grace, whereby we may serve God acceptably with reverence and godly fear: (29) For our God is a consuming fire."

EXODUS 23:25 – KJV. "And ye shall serve the LORD your God, and he shall bless thy bread, and thy water; and I will take sickness away from the midst of thee."

Live in faith and Love.

The Greater Glory is the Manifestation of the Presence, Power, and Goodness of God. (Dr. Jerry Savelle at Living Word Church in Midland, Michigan)

ISAIAH 40:5 – KJV. "And the glory of the LORD shall be revealed, and all flesh shall see it together: for the mouth of the LORD hath spoken it."

ACTS 10:38 – KJV. "How God anointed Jesus of Nazareth with the Holy Ghost and with power: who went about doing good, and healing all that were oppressed of the devil; for God was with him."

Live in the present moment.